Interactive Notebook: Language Arts
Grade 6

Authors: Schyrlet Cameron and Carolyn Craig
Editor: Mary Dieterich
Proofreaders: Margaret Brown and April Albert

ISBN 978-1-62223-761-6

Printing No. CD-405027

Mark Twain Media, Inc., Publishers
Distributed by Carson-Dellosa Publishing LLC

Visit us at www.carsondellosa.com

Table of Contents

To the Teacher

Introduction 1

Organizing an Interactive Notebook 2

Left-hand and Right-hand Notebook Pages 3

Student Handout

Interactive Notebook Grading Rubric 4

Unit One: Sentences

Four Kinds of Sentences 5

Imperative Sentences 7

Subjects and Predicates 9

Compound Subjects and Predicates 11

Conjunctions 13

Unit Two: Nouns

Common and Proper Nouns 15

Plural Nouns 17

Possessive Nouns 19

Nouns as Objects 21

Predicate Nouns 23

Unit Three: Verbs

Action Verbs 25

Helping and Linking Verbs 27

Subject-Verb Agreement 29

Verb Tenses 31

Contractions 33

Unit Four: Adjectives

Adjectives/Proper Adjectives 35

Articles and Demonstrative Adjectives 37

Comparing With Adjectives 39

Five: Adverbs

Adverbs 41

Comparing With Adverbs 43

Unit Six: Prepositions

Prepositions 45

Prepositional Phrases 47

Unit Seven: Pronouns

Pronouns 49

Objective Pronouns 51

Possessive Pronouns 53

Unit Eight: Capitalization and Punctuation

Capitalization 55

Commas 57

Capitalization and Punctuation of Titles 59

Answer Keys 61

Introduction

Interactive Notebook: Language Arts is designed to allow students to become active participants in their own learning. The book lays out an easy-to-follow plan for setting up, creating, and maintaining an interactive notebook.

An interactive notebook is simply a spiral notebook that students use to store and organize important information. It is a culmination of student work throughout the unit of study. Once completed, the notebook becomes the student's own personalized notebook and a great resource for reviewing and studying for tests.

The intent of the book is to help students make sense of new information. Textbooks often present more facts and data than students can process at one time. This book introduces each concept in an easy-to-read and easy-to-understand format that does not overwhelm the learner. The text presents only the most important information, making it easier for students to comprehend. Vocabulary words are printed in boldfaced type.

The book contains 28 lessons covering 8 units of study: Sentences, Nouns, Verbs, Adjectives, Adverbs, Prepositions, Pronouns, and Capitalization and Punctuation. The units can be used in the order presented or in an order that best fits the classroom curriculum. Teachers can easily differentiate units to address the individual learning levels and needs of students. The lessons are designed to support state and national standards. Each lesson consists of two pages.

- **Input page:** essential information for understanding the lesson concepts, directions for creating the interactive page, and extended learning activity.
- **Output page:** hands-on activity such as a foldable or graphic organizer to help students process essential information from the lesson.

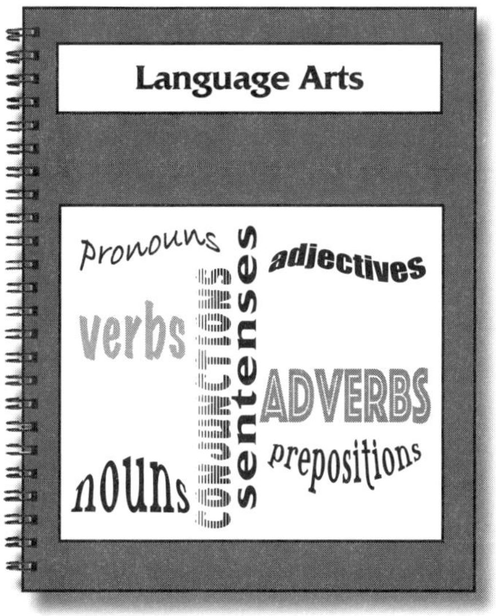

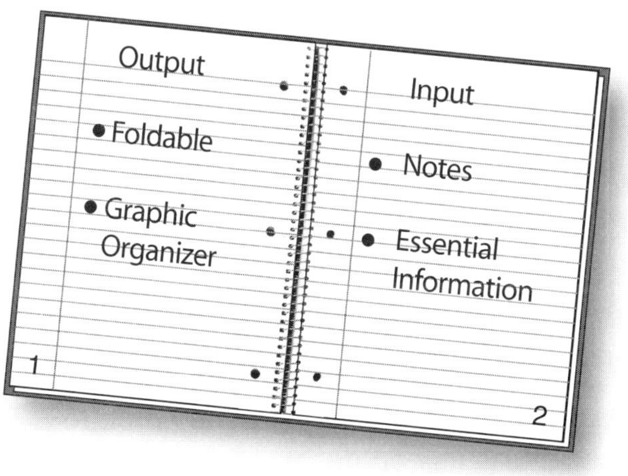

Organizing an Interactive Notebook

What Is an Interactive Notebook?

Does this sound familiar? "I can't find my homework…class notes …study guide." If so, the interactive notebook is a tool you can use to help manage this problem. An interactive notebook is simply a notebook that students use to record, store, and organize their work. The "interactive" aspect of the notebook comes from the fact that students are working with information in various ways as they fill in the notebook. Once completed, the notebook becomes the student's own personalized study guide and a great resource for reviewing information, reinforcing concepts, and studying for tests.

Materials Needed to Create an Interactive Notebook

- Notebook (spiral, composition, or binder with loose-leaf paper)
- Glue stick
- Scissors
- Colored pencils (we do not recommend using markers)
- Tabs

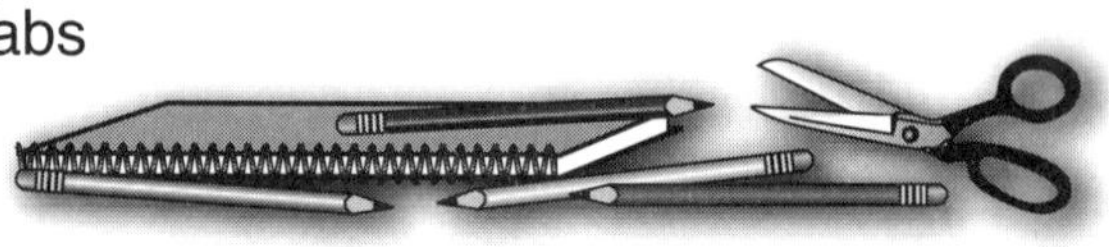

Creating an Interactive Notebook

A good time to introduce the interactive notebook is at the beginning of a new unit of study. Use the following steps to get started.

Step 1: *Notebook Cover*
Students design a cover to reflect the units of study. They should add their names and other important information as directed by the teacher.

Step 2: *Grading Rubric*
Take time to discuss the grading rubric with the students. It is important for each student to understand the expectations for creating the interactive notebook.

Step 3: *Table of Contents*
Students label the first several pages of the notebook "Table of Contents." When completing a new page, they add its title to the table of contents.

Step 4: *Creating Pages*
The notebook is developed using the dual-page format. The right-hand side is the input page where essential information and notes from readings, lectures, or videos are placed. The left-hand side is the output page reserved for foldable activities, charts, graphic organizers, etc. Students number the front and back of each page in the bottom outside corner (odd: LEFT-side; even: RIGHT-side).

Step 5: *Tab Units*
Add a tab to the edge of the first page of each unit to make it easy to flip to the unit.

Step 6: *Glossary*
Students reserve several pages at the back of the notebook where they can create a glossary of domain-specific terms encountered in each lesson.

Step 7: *Pocket*
Students need to attach a pocket to the inside of the back cover of the notebook for storage of handouts, returned quizzes, class syllabus, and other items that don't seem to belong on pages of the notebook. This can be an envelope, resealable plastic bag, or students can design their own pocket.

Left-hand and Right-hand Notebook Pages

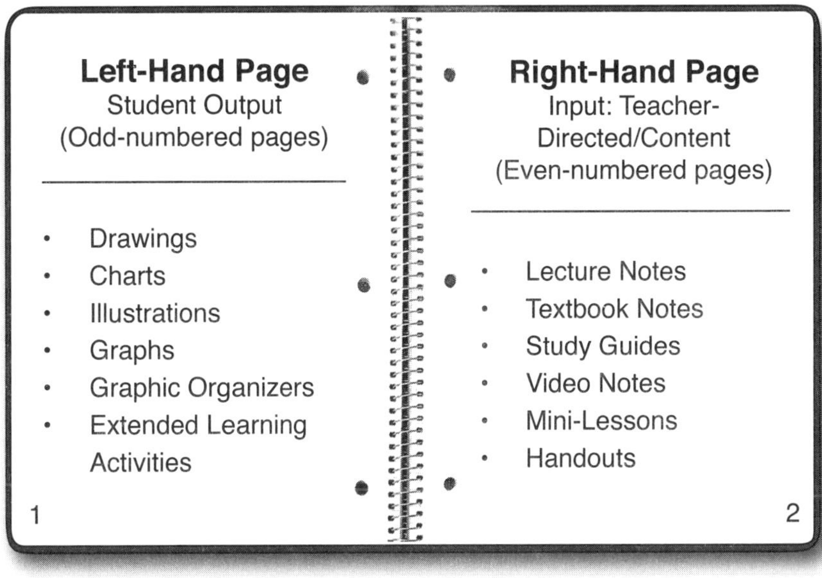

Interactive notebooks are usually viewed open like a textbook. This allows the student to view the left-hand page and right-hand page at the same time. Teachers have several options for how to format the two pages. Traditionally, the right-hand page is used as the input or the content part of the lesson. The left-hand page is the student output part of the lesson. This is where the students have an opportunity to show what they have learned in a creative and colorful way. (Color helps the brain remember information better.) The notebook image on the right details different types of items and activities that could be included on each page.

The format of the interactive notebook involves both the right-brain and left-brain hemispheres to help students process information. When creating the pages, start with the left-hand page. First, have students date the page. Students then move to the right-hand page and the teacher-directed part of the lesson. Finally, students use the information they have learned to complete the left-hand page. Below is an example of completed right- and left-hand pages.

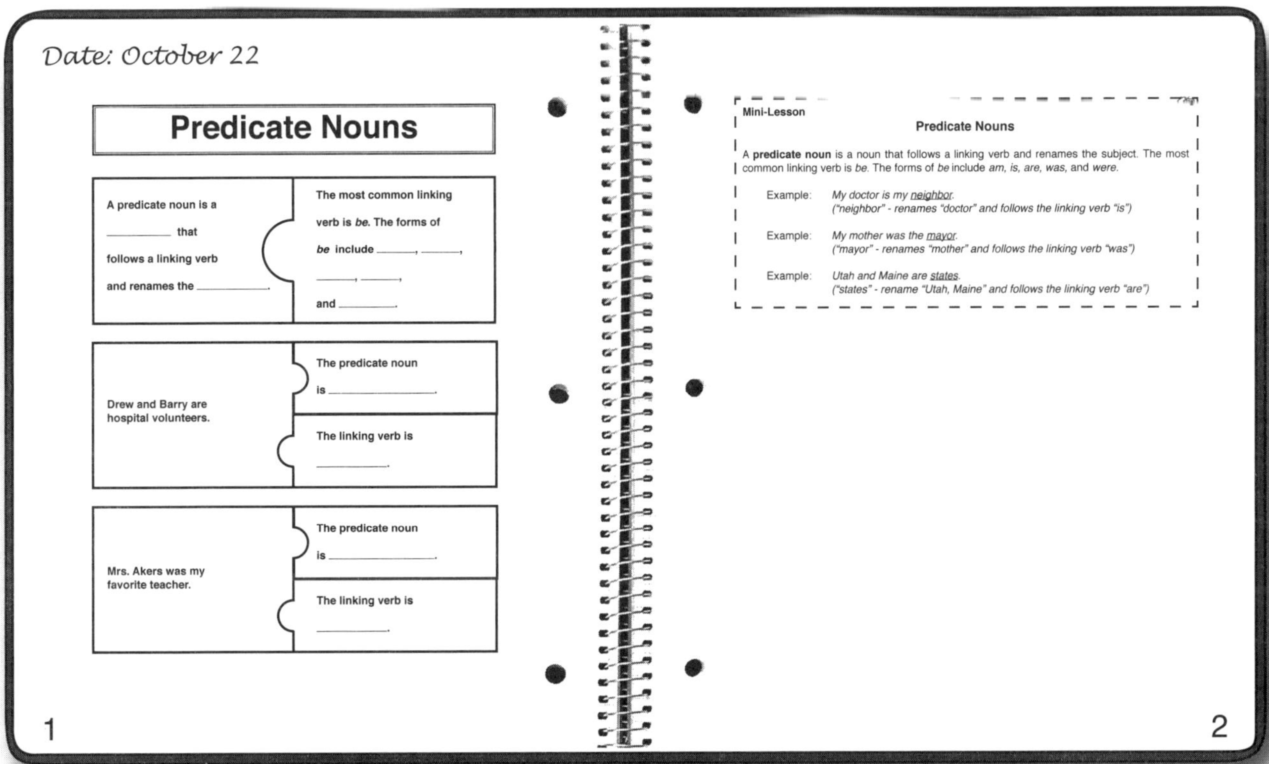

Left-Hand Page **Right-Hand Page**

Interactive Notebook Grading Rubric

Directions: Review the grading rubric below. It lists the criteria that will be used to score your completed interactive notebook. Place this page in your notebook.

Language Arts Interactive Notebook Grading Rubric				
Category	**Excellent (4)**	**Good Work (3)**	**Needs Improvement (2)**	**Incomplete (1)**
Table of Contents	Table of contents is complete.	Table of contents is mostly complete.	Table of contents is somewhat complete.	Attempt was made to include table of contents.
Organization	All pages in correct order. All are numbered, dated, and titled correctly.	Most pages in correct order. Most are numbered, dated, and titled correctly.	Some page in correct order. Some are numbered, dated, and titled correctly.	Few pages in correct order. Few are numbered, dated, and titled correctly.
Content	All information complete, accurate, and placed in the correct order. All spelling correct.	Most information complete, accurate, and placed in the correct order. Most spelling correct.	Some information complete, accurate, and placed in the correct order. Some spelling errors.	Few pages correctly completed. Many spelling errors.
Appearance	All notebook pages are neat and colorful.	Most notebook pages are neat and colorful.	Some notebook pages are neat and colorful.	Few notebook pages are neat and colorful.

Student's Comments:

Teacher's Comments:

Student Instructions: Four Kinds of Sentences

Read the following information. Cut out the mini-lesson and attach it to the right-hand page of your interactive notebook. Use what you have learned to create the left-hand page.

Mini-Lesson

Four Kinds of Sentences

A **sentence** is a group of words that expresses a complete thought. A sentence begins with a capital letter and ends with a punctuation mark. There are four kinds of sentences.

- A **declarative sentence** tells something and ends with a period.
  Example: *Mountains are tall.*
- An **interrogative sentence** asks something and ends with a question mark.
  Example: *Have you been in the mountains?*
- An **imperative sentence** makes a request or gives a command and ends with a period.
  Example: *Be prepared for a change in the oxygen level.*
- An **exclamatory sentence** shows strong feeling and ends with an exclamation point.
  Example: *It was so cold at the top!*

How to Create Your Left-hand Notebook Page

Complete the following steps to create the left-hand page of your notebook.

Step 1: Cut out the title and glue it to the top of the notebook page.
Step 2: Fill in the blanks on the *Sentence Definition* piece. Cut out the piece and apply glue to the back. Attach it below the title.
Step 3: Cut out the puzzle flaps. Match each sentence name with the correct definition. Apply glue to the back of the gray tabs and attach the matched puzzle flaps below the definition piece.
Step 4: Under each set of matched puzzle flaps, write an example of the type of sentence.

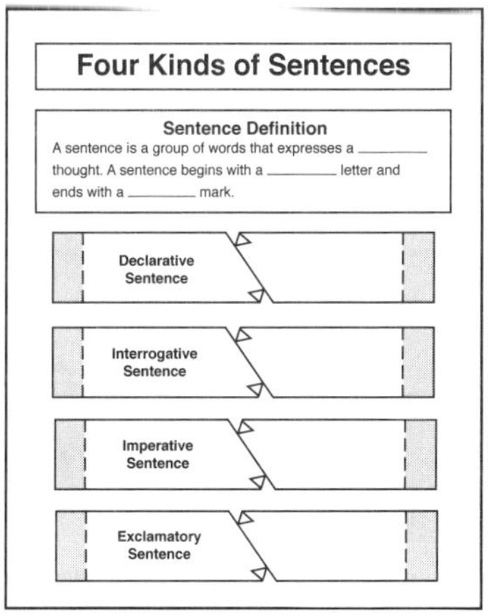

Demonstrate What You Have Learned

Find an example of each type of sentence in print material such as newspapers and magazines. Cut out the sentences and glue them in your interactive notebook. Label each type of sentence.

Four Kinds of Sentences

Sentence Definition

A sentence is a group of words that expresses a ____________________ thought. A sentence begins with a ______________________ letter and ends with a ________________________ mark.

Declarative Sentence	**A sentence that asks something and ends with a question mark.**
Interrogative Sentence	**A sentence that shows strong feeling and ends with an exclamation point.**
Imperative Sentence	**A sentence that tells something and ends with a period.**
Exclamatory Sentence	**A sentence that makes a request or gives a command and ends with a period.**

Student Instructions: Imperative Sentences

Read the following information. Cut out the mini-lesson and attach it to the right-hand page of your interactive notebook. Use what you have learned to create the left-hand page.

Mini-Lesson

Imperative Sentences

An **imperative sentence** makes a request or gives a command and ends with a period. Some commands can be written with the subject "you" missing. It is understood to be in the sentence.

Example: *You should leave the house earlier.* (Request)

Leave the house earlier. (Command with *You* as the understood subject)

Sally, pick up your socks. (Command; subject is *Sally*)

How to Create Your Left-Hand Notebook Page

Complete the following steps to create the left-hand page of your notebook.

Step 1: Cut out the title and glue it to the top of the notebook page.

Step 2: Cut out the *Imperative Sentences* flap book. Cut on the solid lines to create six flaps. Apply glue to the back of the gray center section. Attach the flap book below the title.

Step 3: Under each flap, rewrite the imperative sentences to commands with the understood you.

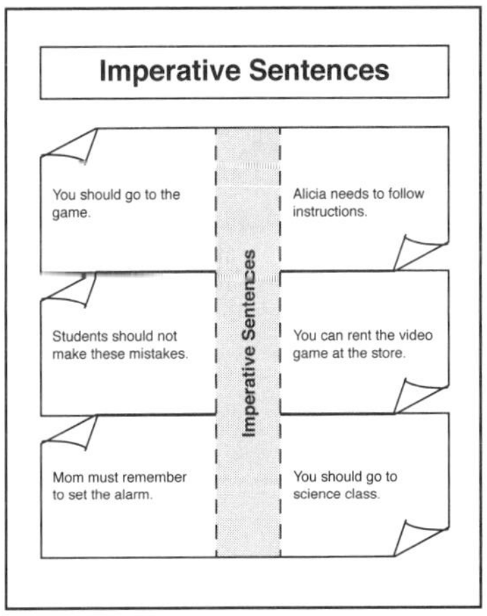

Demonstrate What You Have Learned

Think about your day. In your interactive notebook, write five command sentences you heard spoken by your parents, teachers, classmates, and friends.

Imperative Sentences

	Imperative Sentences	
You should go to the game.		Alicia needs to follow instructions.
Students should not make these mistakes.		You can rent the video game at the store.
Mom must remember to set the alarm.		You should go to science class.

Student Instructions: Subjects and Predicates

Read the following information. Cut out the mini-lesson and attach it to the right-hand page of your interactive notebook. Use what you have learned to create the left-hand page.

Mini-Lesson

Subjects and Predicates

Subject and Predicate

Every sentence has two parts, a subject and a predicate. A **subject** tells whom or what the sentence is about. The **predicate** tells what the subject is or does.

Example:	**Subject**	**Predicate**
	Birds	*sang.*

Complete Subject and Complete Predicate

The **complete subject** contains the subject (what the sentence is about) and all the words that go with it. The **simple subject** is the main noun or pronoun in the complete subject. The **complete predicate** contains the verb and all the words that go with it. The **simple predicate** is the verb or verb phrase in the complete predicate.

Example:	**Complete Subject**	**Complete Predicate**
	The beautiful bald eagle	*is a natural symbol of the United States.*

How to Create Your Left-hand Notebook Page

Complete the following steps to create the left-hand page of your notebook.

Step 1: Cut out the title and glue it to the top of the notebook page.

Step 2: Cut out the two *What is the Difference?* flap books. Apply glue to the back of the gray center sections and attach the flap books below the title. Write the definition under each flap.

Step 3: Complete the chart by writing "complete subject" or "complete predicate" to describe the underlined part of each sentence.

Step 4: Apply glue to the back of the chart and attach it at the bottom of the page.

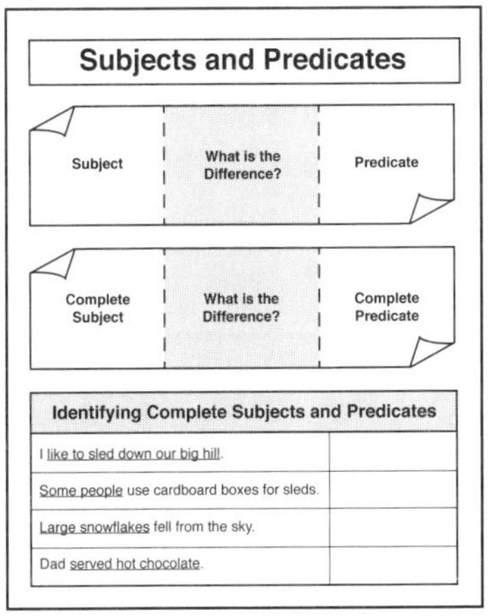

Demonstrate What You Have Learned

Copy the sentences below in your interactive notebook. Underline the complete subject once and the complete predicate twice. Draw a box around the simple subject and circle the simple predicate.

1. My sister has the flu.
2. The Norton family is vacationing in New York.

Subjects and Predicates

Subject	What is the Difference?	Predicate

Complete Subject	What is the Difference?	Complete Predicate

Identifying Complete Subjects and Predicates	
I <u>like to sled down our big hill</u>.	
<u>Some people</u> use cardboard boxes for sleds.	
<u>Large snowflakes</u> fell from the sky.	
Dad <u>served hot chocolate</u>.	

Student Instructions: Compound Subjects and Predicates

Read the following information. Cut out the mini-lesson and attach it to the right-hand page of your interactive notebook. Use what you have learned to create the left-hand page.

Mini-Lesson

Compound Subjects and Predicates

A **compound subject** is two or more subjects that share a predicate. The subjects are joined by a conjunction, or a connecting word, such as *and, or,* or *but.*

Examples: *Planes and trains are types of transportation.*
Either Tony or José is going to get the job.

A **compound predicate** is two or more predicates that share the same subject. The predicates are joined by a conjunction, or a connecting word, such as *and, or,* or *but.*

Examples: *The dog scratched and barked at the door.*
Many people neither enjoy nor appreciate the theater.

How to Create Your Left-hand Notebook Page

Complete the following steps to create the left-hand page of your notebook.

Step 1: Cut out the title and glue it to the top of the notebook page.

Step 2: Fill in the blanks on the Compound Subjects and Predicates pockets. Cut out the two pockets. Fold back the gray tabs on the dotted lines. Apply glue to the tabs and attach each pocket below the title.

Step 3: Cut apart the sentence strips. Place each strip in the correct pocket.

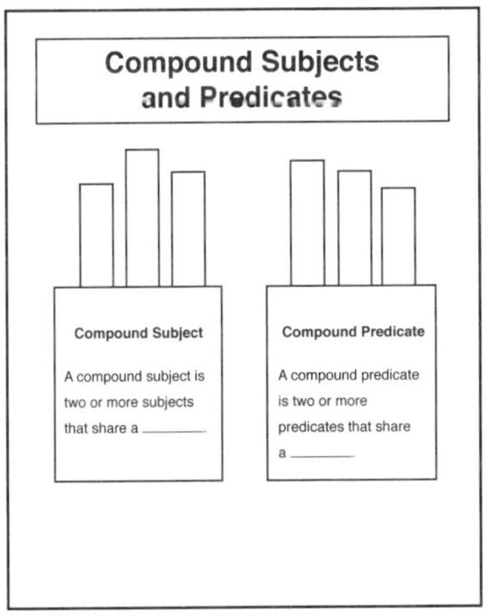

Demonstrate What You Have Learned

In your interactive notebook, write a sentence of your own using both the compound subjects and the compound predicates provided.

Compound Subjects	**Compound Predicates**
Tara; Josh	stayed; studied

Compound Subjects and Predicates

Compound Subject

A compound subject is two or more subjects that share a ___________.

Compound Predicate

A compound predicate is two or more predicates that share a ___________.

The team worked and finished their science project.
Marie always laughed or cried at dramatic plays.
Neither chips nor sodas are healthy after-school snacks.
The window or door has to be closed.
Steve competed but lost the race.
Brian and Kendra went to the beach during spring break.

Student Instructions: Conjunctions

Read the following information. Cut out the mini-lesson and attach it to the right-hand page of your interactive notebook. Use what you have learned to create the left-hand page.

Mini-Lesson

Conjunctions

A **conjunction** is a word used to join words, phrases, and sentences. The most common conjunctions include the words *and, but, or, yet, for,* and *so.*

Example: *Ants crawled over the blanket and into the picnic basket.*

The hero is a good person, but the villain is not.

Did they travel by plane or train to Seattle, Washington?

I hate to waste a bite of food, for it is very expensive these days.

I am allergic to dogs, yet I have two bulldogs.

My friend is a vegetarian, so she does not eat any meat.

How to Create Your Left-hand Notebook Page

Complete the following steps to create the left-hand page of your notebook.

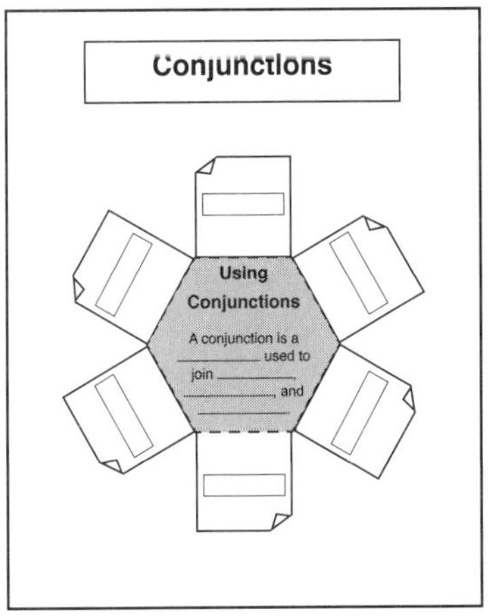

Step 1: Cut out the title and glue it to the top of the notebook page.

Step 2: Fill in the blanks in the *Using Conjunctions* flap book then cut out the flap book. Apply glue to the back of the gray center section and attach the flap book below the title.

Step 3: Cut out the six conjunction pieces. Apply glue to the back of each piece. Attach a conjunction to each flap.

Step 4: Under each flap, write a sentence using the conjunction.

Demonstrate What You Have Learned

Look in your favorite fiction book for sentences containing each of the common conjunctions. Write the title of the book in your interactive notebook. Copy the sentences below the title.

Conjunctions

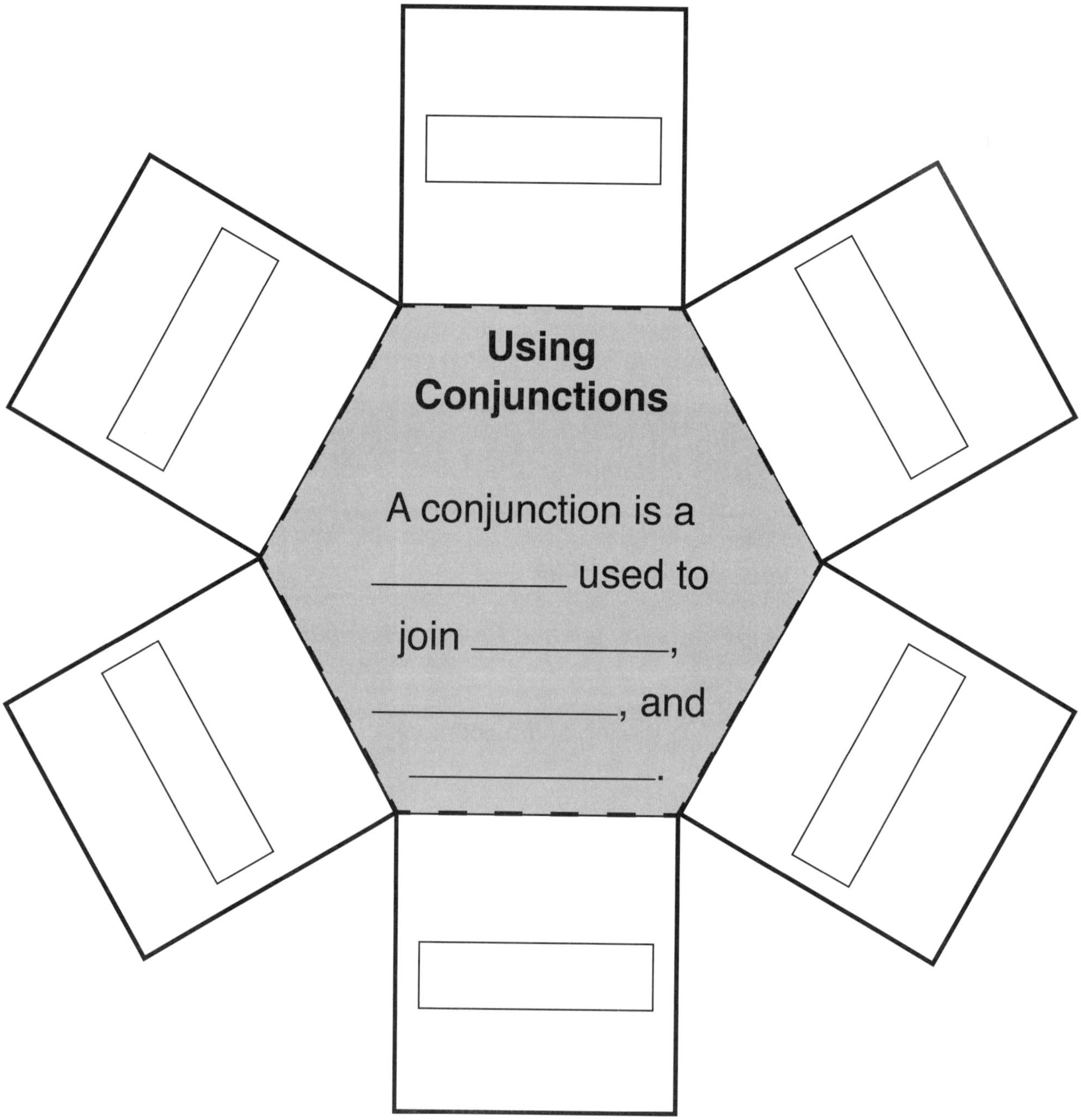

and	or	but
yet	for	so

Student Instructions: Common and Proper Nouns

Read the following information. Cut out the mini-lesson and attach it to the right-hand page of your interactive notebook. Use what you have learned to create the left-hand page.

Mini-Lesson

Common and Proper Nouns

A **noun** names a person, place, or thing. Nouns can be common or proper. A **common noun** names any person, place, or thing. A **proper noun** names a particular person, place, or thing. Proper nouns are always capitalized.

Examples:	Common Nouns	Proper Nouns
	language	*English*
	dog	*Rover*
	month	*June*
	holiday	*Earth Day*
	country	*Mexico*
	doctor	*Dr. Evans*
	river	*Mississippi River*

How to Create Your Left-hand Notebook Page

Complete the following steps to create the left-hand page of your notebook.

Step 1: Cut out the title and glue it to the top of the notebook page.

Step 2: Fill in the blanks on the *Common Noun* and *Proper Noun* pieces. Cut out the pieces and apply glue to the backs. Attach the pieces below the title.

Step 3: Cut apart the eight word pieces. Attach each piece below the noun piece that describes it.

Demonstrate What You Have Learned

Draw the chart to the right in your interactive notebook. Write a proper noun for each common noun listed.

Nouns	
Common Nouns	**Proper Nouns**
city	
mountain	
business	
ocean	
state	

Common and Proper Nouns

Pacific Ocean	**woman**	**town**	**Blue Mountains**
cat	**Pizza Place**	**Spanish**	**restaurant**

Student Instructions: Plural Nouns

Read the following information. Cut out the mini-lesson and attach it to the right-hand page of your interactive notebook. Use what you have learned to create the left-hand page.

Mini-Lesson

Plural Nouns

Singular nouns name one person, place, or thing. **Plural nouns** name more than one person, place, or thing.

Rules for forming plural nouns vary.

- Most singular nouns add "s" to form plurals.
  Example: *house/houses* *street/streets*
- Nouns ending in *s, x, ch,* and *sh* add "es" to form plurals.
  Example: *dress/dresses* *ax/axes* *church/churches* *dish/dishes*
- Nouns ending with a vowel and *y* add "s" to form plurals.
  Example: *valley/valleys* *joy/joys*
- Nouns ending in a consonant and *y* change the *y* to "i" and add "es" to form plurals.
  Example: *city/cities* *berry/berries*

How to Create Your Left-hand Notebook Page

Complete the following steps to create the left-hand page of your notebook.

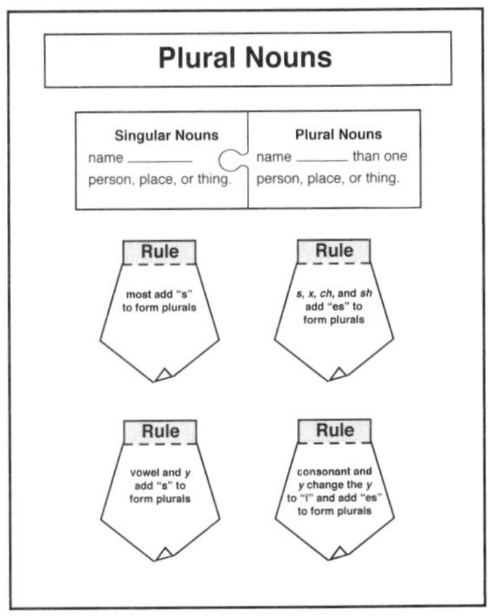

Step 1: Cut out the title and glue it to the top of the notebook page.
Step 2: Fill in the blanks on the *Singular Nouns* and *Plural Nouns* puzzle piece. Cut out the piece. Apply glue to the back and attach the piece below the title.
Step 3: Cut out the four *Rule* flap pieces. Apply glue to the back of each gray tab. Attach the flap pieces at the bottom of the page. Under each flap, write an example for the rule.

Demonstrate What You Have Learned

Think about the rules for forming plural nouns. In your interactive notebook, write a sentence using each of the plural forms of the nouns below.

1. desk 2. piano 3. leaf

Plural Nouns

Singular Nouns	**Plural Nouns**
name ____________ person, place, or thing.	name ____________ than one person, place, or thing.

Rule

most add "s" to form plurals

Rule

***s, x, ch,* and *sh* add "es" to form plurals**

Rule

vowel and *y* add "s" to form plurals

Rule

consonant and *y* change the *y* to "i" and add "es" to form plurals

Student Instructions: Possessive Nouns

Read the following information. Cut out the mini-lesson and attach it to the right-hand page of your interactive notebook. Use what you have learned to create the left-hand page.

Mini-Lesson

Possessive Nouns

A **singular possessive noun** shows that one person, place, or thing has or owns something. Form a singular possessive noun by adding an apostrophe (') and "s" to the singular noun.

Examples:	**Singular Noun**	**Singular Possessive Noun**
	a boy owns a bike	*a boy's bike*

A **plural possessive noun** shows that more than one person, place, or thing has or owns something. To form the plural possessive of a plural noun that ends in "s," add only an apostrophe. If the plural noun does not end in "s," add an apostrophe (') and "s."

Examples:	**Plural**	**Plural Possessive**
	boys have hats	*boys' hats*
	babies have food	*babies' food*
	men own cars	*men's cars*

How to Create Your Left-hand Notebook Page

Complete the following steps to create the left-hand page of your notebook.

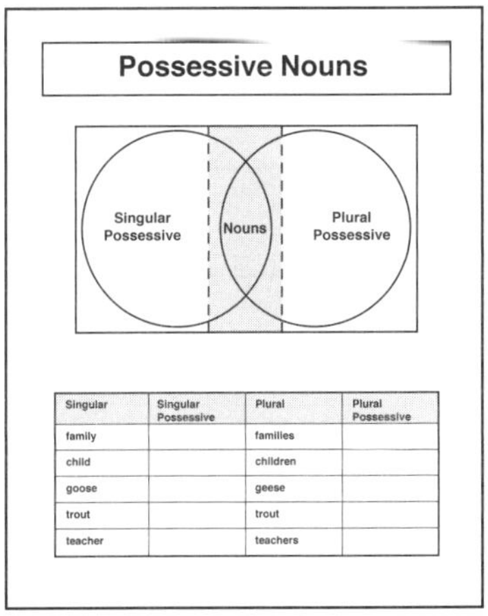

Step 1: Cut out the title and glue it to the top of the notebook page.
Step 2: Cut out the *Nouns* Venn diagram flap book. Apply glue to the gray center section and attach the flap book below the title. Under each flap, write the definition.
Step 3: Cut out the chart and apply glue to the back. Attach the chart at the bottom of the page.
Step 4: Cut apart the ten word pieces. Glue each piece in the correct box on the chart.

Demonstrate What You Have Learned

Write three sentences using the word *pony*. Write one sentence using the singular possessive form, one sentence using the plural form, one sentence using the plural possessive form of the word.

Possessive Nouns

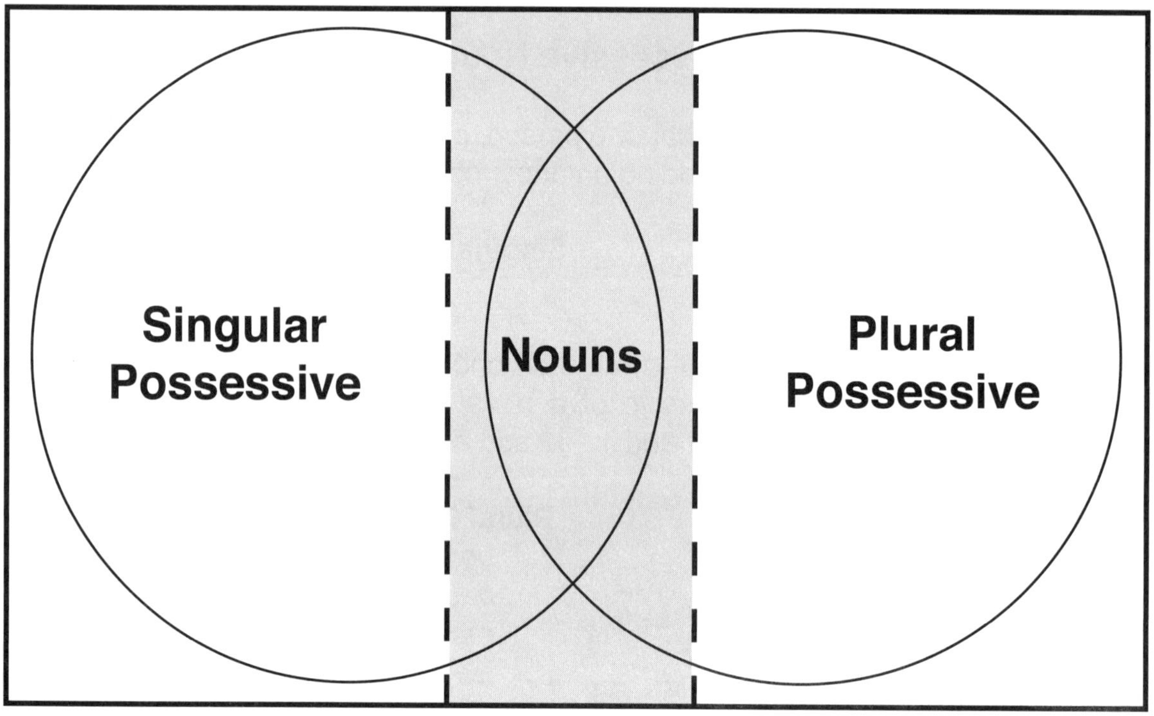

Singular	Singular Possessive	Plural	Plural Possessive
family		families	
child		children	
goose		geese	
trout		trout	
teacher		teachers	

trout's	teacher's	children's	families'	geese's
child's	family's	goose's	trout's	teachers'

Student Instructions: Nouns as Objects

Read the following information. Cut out the mini-lesson and attach it to the right-hand page of your interactive notebook. Use what you have learned to create the left-hand page.

Mini-Lesson

Nouns as Objects

A **noun** is a word that names a person, place or thing. Nouns can be used as subjects of sentences. Other times, however, nouns can be used as direct objects. A **direct object** (**D.O.**) is a noun that follows an **action verb** (**A.V.**). It answers the question "who?" or "what?" about the verb to complete the meaning of the sentence.

Example: *The Andersons built a new house.* **Question:** *The Andersons built what?*
A.V. D.O. **Answer:** *"house" (direct object)*

Some nouns can be indirect objects. An **indirect object** (**I.O.**) is a noun that comes between the verb and the direct object (D.O.). The indirect object answers the question "to whom?" or "for whom?" the action of the verb is performed. It answers the question "to what?" and "for what?" something is done.

Example: *I told my granddaughter a story.* **Question:** *What did I tell?*
S V I.O. D.O. **Answer:** *"story" (direct object)*
Question: *To whom did I tell?*
Answer: *"granddaughter" (indirect object)*

How to Create Your Left-hand Notebook Page

Complete the following steps to create the left-hand page of your notebook.

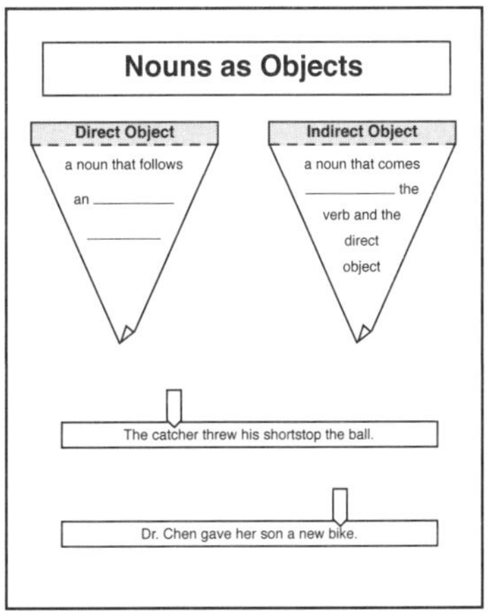

Step 1: Cut out the title and glue it to the top of the notebook page.
Step 2: Fill in the blanks on the *Direct Object* and *Indirect Object* pieces. Apply glue to the back of each gray tab and attach the pieces below the title. Under each flap, write a sentence demonstrating the rule.
Step 3: Cut out the two sentence strips. Apply glue to the back of each strip. Attach the strips at the bottom of the page. Be sure to leave room between the sentence strips.
Step 4: Cut out the six word pieces. Apply glue to the back of each piece. Attach each piece above the word in the sentence that it describes.

Demonstrate What You Have Learned

Copy the two sentences in your interactive notebook. Label each sentence with an **S** for the subject, **A.V.** for the action verb, and **D.O.** for the direct object.

1. Tony accepted the batting trophy.
2. The caterpillars make cocoons.

Nouns as Objects

Direct Object

a noun that follows

an ______________

____

Indirect Object

a noun that comes

______________ the

verb and the

direct

object

Subject

Subject

Direct Object

Indirect Object

Indirect Object

Direct Object

The catcher threw his shortstop the ball.

Dr. Chen gave her son a new bike.

Predicate Nouns

Read the following information. Cut out the mini-lesson and attach it to the right-hand page of your interactive notebook. Use what you have learned to create the left-hand page.

Mini-Lesson

Predicate Nouns

A **predicate noun** is a noun that follows a linking verb and renames the subject. The most common linking verb is *be*. The forms of *be* include *am, is, are, was,* and *were.*

Example: *My doctor is my <u>neighbor</u>.*
("neighbor" - renames "doctor" and follows the linking verb "is")

Example: *My mother was the <u>mayor</u>.*
("mayor" - renames "mother" and follows the linking verb "was")

Example: *Utah and Maine are <u>states</u>.*
("states" - renames "Utah, Maine" and follows the linking verb "are")

How to Create Your Left-hand Notebook Page

Complete the following steps to create the left-hand page of your notebook.

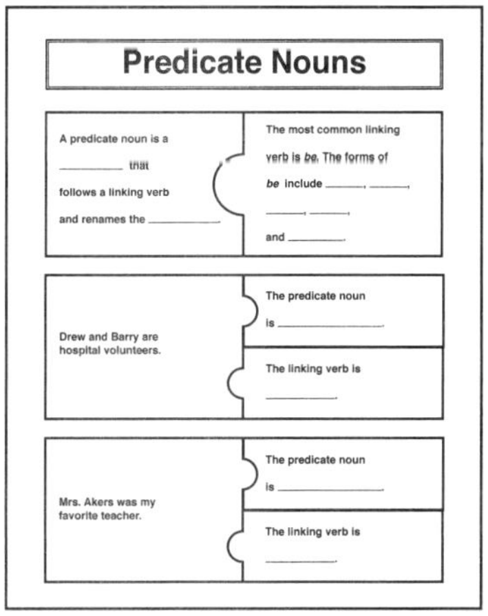

Step 1: Cut out the title and glue it to the top of the notebook page.

Step 2: Fill in the blanks on the puzzle pieces. Cut out the pieces and apply glue to the back. Attach the pieces below the title.

Demonstrate What You Have Learned

In your interactive notebook, write five sentences about school. Use a predicate noun in each sentence. Label the subject (**S**), linking verb (**L.V.**), and predicate noun (**P.N.**) in each sentence.

Predicate Nouns

A predicate noun is a ________ that follows a linking verb and renames the ________.

The most common linking verb is *be*. The forms of *be* include ______, ______, ______, ______, and ______.

Drew and Barry are hospital volunteers.

The predicate noun is ________.

The linking verb is ________.

Mrs. Akers was my favorite teacher.

The predicate noun is ________.

The linking verb is ________.

Student Instructions: Action Verbs

Read the following information. Cut out the mini-lesson and attach it to the right-hand page of your interactive notebook. Use what you have learned to create the left-hand page.

Mini-Lesson

Action Verbs

A **verb** is a word or words in the predicate that tell what the subject of a sentence is or does. An **action verb** is a word that expresses physical or mental action. Most action verbs show physical actions you can see, such as *run, cook,* and *jump*. Some verbs, such as *think* and *want,* show mental actions you cannot see.

Examples: *The hockey player scored the winning goal.*
My sister waters the flowers.
Senator Smith thinks the bill will pass.

Common Action Verbs

agree	*drink*	*help*	*laugh*	*put*	*think*
ask	*eat*	*hop*	*leave*	*push*	*use*
bring	*exit*	*insult*	*lift*	*read*	*visit*
buy	*fall*	*joke*	*march*	*ride*	*vote*
call	*fix*	*jump*	*move*	*send*	*wait*
close	*give*	*keep*	*nod*	*spend*	*write*
dream	*grab*	*kick*	*open*	*talk*	*yell*

How to Create Your Left-hand Notebook Page

Complete the following steps to create the left-hand page of your notebook.

Step 1: Cut out the title and glue it to the top of the notebook page.

Step 2: Fill in the blanks on the *Action Verb* flap book then cut out the flap book. Apply glue to the back of the gray center section. Attach the flap book below the title.

Step 3: Under each flap, write a sentence with an action verb to describe the picture. Underline the action verb.

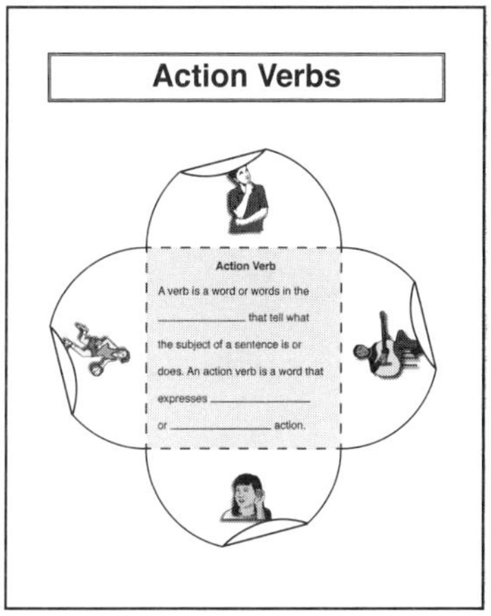

Demonstrate What You Have Learned

Write a list of 50 action verbs in your interactive notebook. Include words that express physical action and words that express mental action. If you need help, use online or print resources.

Action Verbs

Action Verb

A verb is a word or words in the ________________ that tell what the subject of a sentence is or does. An action verb is a word that expresses ________________ or ________________ action.

Student Instructions: Helping and Linking Verbs

Read the following information. Cut out the mini-lesson and attach it to the right-hand page of your interactive notebook. Use what you have learned to create the left-hand page.

Mini-Lesson

Helping and Linking Verbs

A **helping verb** comes before the main verb. It works with the main verb to form a verb phrase.

Common Helping Verbs

am	*are*	*were*	*shall*	*has*	*is*	*was*
will	*have*	*had*				

Example: *Our garden is growing rapidly.*

A **linking verb** joins the subject to a word in the predicate that names or describes the subject. It does not show action. It does not act as a helping verb.

Common Linking Verbs

am	*is*	*are*	*was*	*look*	*feel*	*taste*
smell	*were*	*seem*	*will be*	*appear*		

Example: *Sue is a cheerleader.*
("cheerleader"- renames "Sue" and follows the linking verb "is")

How to Create Your Left-hand Notebook Page

Complete the following steps to create the left-hand page of your notebook.

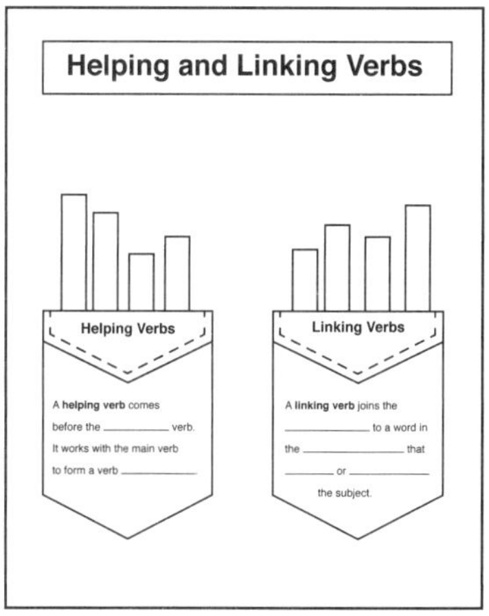

Step 1: Cut out the title and glue it to the top of the notebook page.
Step 2: Fill in the blanks on the *Helping Verbs* and the *Linking Verbs* pockets. Cut out the two pockets. Fold back the gray tabs on the dotted lines. Apply glue to the tabs and attach each pocket below the title.
Step 3: Cut apart the sentence strips. Place each strip in the correct pocket.

Demonstrate What You Have Learned

Write three sentences in your interactive notebook that follow the directions below.

1. Write a sentence that uses the word *were* as a linking verb.
2. Write a sentence that uses the word *was* as a helping verb.
3. Write a sentence that uses the word *drink* with a helping verb.

Helping and Linking Verbs

Helping Verbs

A **helping verb** comes before the ________ verb. It works with the main verb to form a verb ________.

Linking Verbs

A **linking verb** joins the ____________ to a word in the ______________ that ________ or ________ the subject.

1. My family has ordered tickets already.	5. Tomas is a scientist.
2. Monday will be my birthday.	6. The neighbors are visiting relatives.
3. My sister is going to college.	7. We were studying for the test.
4. The people in line were impatient.	8. Coleen is the class president.

Student Instructions: Subject-Verb Agreement

Read the following information. Cut out the mini-lesson and attach it to the right-hand page of your interactive notebook. Use what you have learned to create the left-hand page.

Mini-Lesson

Subject-Verb Agreement

The subject of a sentence and the verb must work together. This means both need to be singular or both need to be plural. A **singular subject** must have a singular verb. Add "s" or "es" to the verb if the subject is singular. A **plural subject** must have a plural verb. Do not add "s" or "es" to the verb if the subject is plural or if the subject is *I* or *you.*

- **Singular Subject**
  Example: *He teaches; Man fishes* *(add "s" or "es")*
- **Plural Subject**
  Example: *Cats play; Men fish* *(do not add "s" or "es")*
- **Subject is *I* or *you***
  Example: *I like; You fish* *(do not add "s" or "es")*
- **Subject is *we, they, several, few,* or *many***
  Example: *We run; Many fly* *(do not add "s" or "es")*

How to Create Your Left-hand Notebook Page

Complete the following steps to create the left-hand page of your notebook.

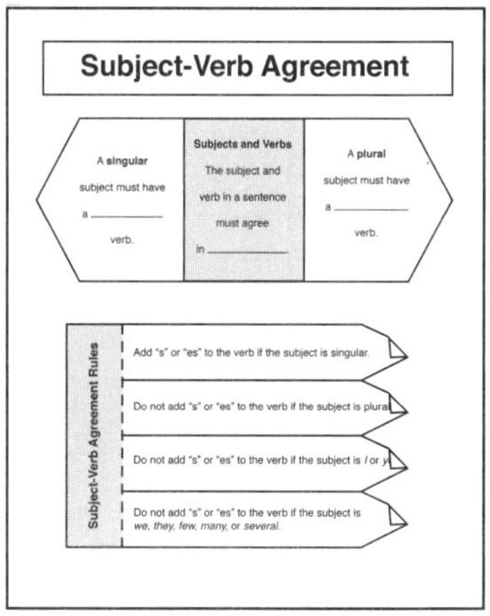

Step 1: Cut out the title and glue it to the top of the notebook page.

Step 2: Fill in the blanks on the *Subjects and Verbs* piece. Cut out the piece and apply glue to the back. Attach the piece below the title.

Step 3: Cut out the *Subject-Verb Agreement Rules* flap book. Cut on the solid lines to create four flaps. Under each flap, write a sentence that follows the rule.

Demonstrate What You Have Learned

What is it that makes you happy? Why? In your interactive notebook, write about those things and tell why. Make subjects and verbs agree.

Subject-Verb Agreement

A **singular** subject must have a ____________ verb.

Subjects and Verbs

The subject and verb in a sentence must agree in ____________.

A **plural** subject must have a ____________ verb.

Subject-Verb Agreement Rules

- Add "s" or "es" to the verb if the subject is singular.
- Do not add "s" or "es" to the verb if the subject is plural.
- Do not add "s" or "es" to the verb if the subject is *I* or *you.*
- Do not add "s" or "es" to the verb if the subject is *we, they, few, many,* or *several.*

Student Instructions: Verb Tenses

Read the following information. Cut out the mini-lesson and attach it to the right-hand page of your interactive notebook. Use what you have learned to create the left-hand page.

Mini-Lesson

Verb Tenses

The **tense** of a **verb** tells when a person did something or when something existed or happened. There are three verb tenses: present, past, and future.

- **Present tense verbs** show action that happens now.
  Example: *Lori draws great cartoons.*
- **Past tense verbs** show action that has already happened.
  Example: *Lori drew cartoons yesterday.*
- **Future tense verbs** show action that will happen.
  Example: *Lori will draw more cartoons.*

How to Create Your Left-hand Notebook Page

Complete the following steps to create the left-hand page of your notebook.

Step 1: Cut out the title and glue it to the top of the notebook page.

Step 2: Cut out the arrow flap pieces. Match up the tense and the definition pieces. Apply glue to the back of the gray tabs and glue the matched pieces below the title.

Step 3: Under each matched piece, write a sentence using the correct tense. Underline the verb in each sentence.

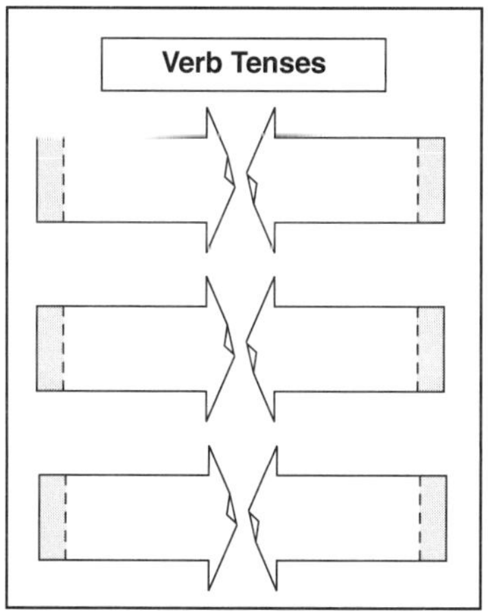

Demonstrate What You Have Learned

Create a chart like the one to the right in your interactive notebook. Write sentences using the present, past, and future tenses for the two verbs listed in the chart.

leave	
Present	
Past	
Future	
study	
Present	
Past	
Future	

Verb Tenses

Present Tense Verb

shows action that has already happened

Past Tense Verb

shows action that will happen

Future Tense Verb

shows action that happens now

Student Instructions: Contractions

Read the following information. Cut out the mini-lesson and attach it to the right-hand page of your interactive notebook. Use what you have learned to create the left-hand page.

Mini-Lesson

Contractions

A **contraction** is a word formed by joining two words, making one word shorter. An apostrophe (') is used in place of any missing letters in contractions.

Examples: *It's* is a contraction for *it is.*
We've is a contraction for *we have.*

Some contractions are made with a verb plus the word *not*.

Example: *do not—don't* *have not—haven't* *is not—isn't*

The word *not* is not a verb. It cannot be part of a verb phrase. Therefore, the "n't" in a contraction cannot be part of a verb phrase.

Example: *The pitcher hasn't allowed a run yet.*
Verb phrase—has allowed

How to Create Your Left-hand Notebook Page

Complete the following steps to create the left-hand page of your notebook.

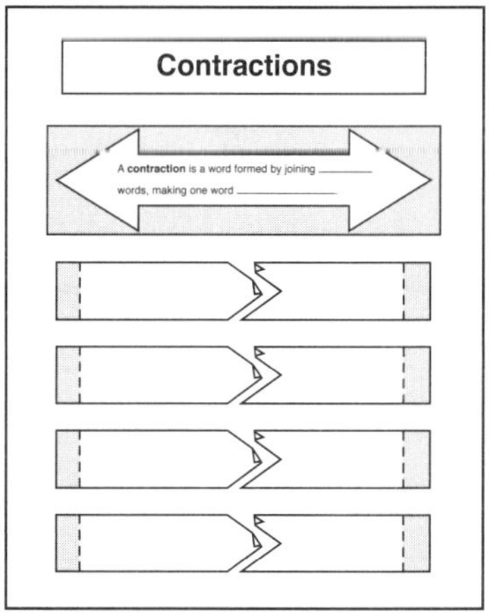

Step 1: Cut out the title and glue it to the top of the notebook page.

Step 2: Fill in the blanks on the Contraction Definition piece. Cut out the piece and apply glue to the back. Attach it below the title.

Step 3: Cut out the puzzle flaps. Match each two-word piece with the correct contraction. Apply glue to the back of the gray tabs and attach the matched puzzle flaps below the contraction pieces.

Step 4: Under each set of matched puzzle flaps, write the missing letters that the apostrophe was used for, and write a sentence using the contraction.

Demonstrate What You Have Learned

Copy the sentences below in your interactive notebook. Circle the contraction and write the correct verb phrase beneath each sentence.

1. Manuel didn't call me last night.
2. I don't like watermelon.

Contractions

A **contraction** is a word formed by joining ________ words, making one word ________.

does not	**she'd**
I will	**doesn't**
she would	**I'll**
you are	**you're**

Student Instructions: Adjectives/Proper Adjectives

Read the following information. Cut out the mini-lesson and attach it to the right-hand page of your interactive notebook. Use what you have learned to create the left-hand page.

Mini-Lesson

Adjectives/Proper Adjectives

An **adjective** is a word that describes a noun or pronoun. Adjectives tell "what kind," "how many," or "which one."

- **"what kind"**
  Examples: *They served fresh fruit.* *Our team looked tired.*
- **"how many"**
  Examples: *Four boys played golf.* *Several people left early.*
- **"which one"**
  Examples: *Those flowers are from Dave.* *I have read that book.*

A **proper adjective** is formed from a proper noun and begins with a capital letter.

Example:	**Proper Noun**	**Proper Adjective**
	Italy	*Italian food*

How to Create Your Left-hand Notebook Page

Complete the following steps to create the left-hand page of your notebook.

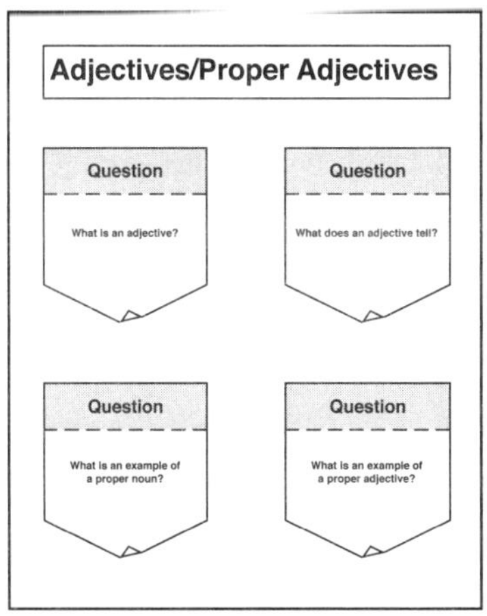

Step 1: Cut out the title and glue it to the top of the notebook page.

Step 2: Cut out the four *Question* flap pieces. Apply glue to the back of the gray tabs and attach each flap piece below the title.

Step 3: Under each flap, write the answer to the question.

Adjectives	
Proper Nouns	**Proper Adjectives**
Russia	
Denmark	
Alaska	
Turkey	
Greece	

Demonstrate What You Have Learned

Draw the chart to the left in your interactive notebook. Write a proper adjective for each proper noun listed.

Adjectives/Proper Adjectives

Question

What is an adjective?

Question

What does an adjective tell?

Question

What is an example of a proper noun?

Question

What is an example of a proper adjective?

Student Instructions: Articles and Demonstrative Adjectives

Read the following information. Cut out the mini-lesson and attach it to the right-hand page of your interactive notebook. Use what you have learned to create the left-hand page.

Mini-Lesson

Articles and Demonstrative Adjectives

A, an, and *the* are special adjectives called **articles**. The articles *a* and *an* are used only with singular nouns. Use *a* before words that begin with a consonant sound. Use *an* before words that begin with a vowel sound or a silent "h."

Examples: *a jungle; an egg; the plans; a big contest; an honest boy*

Demonstrative adjectives tell "which one." The adjectives *this* and *these* refer to things nearby. The adjectives *that* and *those* refer to things farther away.

How to Create Your Left-hand Notebook Page

Complete the following steps to create the left-hand page of your notebook.

Step 1: Cut out the title and glue it to the top of the notebook page.

Step 2: Fill in the blanks on the *Articles* and *Demonstrative Adjectives* pockets. Cut out the two pockets. Fold back the gray tabs on the dotted lines. Apply glue to the tabs and attach each pocket below the title.

Step 3: On the four blank strips, write two sentences for each pocket that demonstrate the rule. Cut out the sentence strips. Place each strip in the correct pocket.

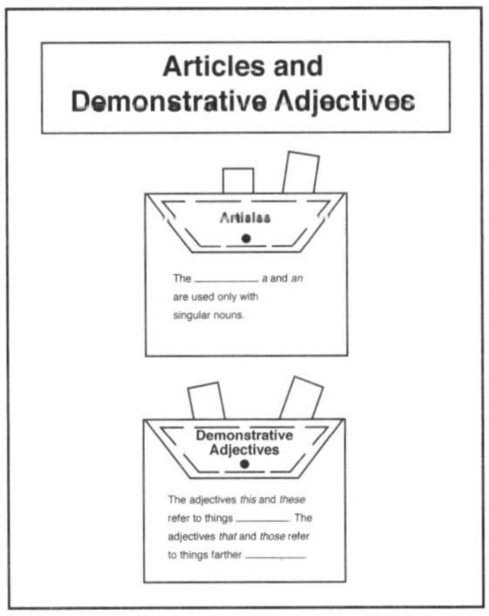

Demonstrate What You Have Learned

In your interactive notebook, write a paragraph about your favorite song. Use articles and demonstrative adjectives in your paragraph. Underline all the articles and demonstrative adjectives that you use.

Articles and Demonstrative Adjectives

Articles

The __________ *a* and *an* are used only with singular nouns.

Demonstrative Adjectives

The adjectives *this* and *these* refer to things __________. The adjectives *that* and *those* refer to things farther __________.

Student Instructions: Comparing With Adjectives

Read the following information. Cut out the mini-lesson and attach it to the right-hand page of your interactive notebook. Use what you have learned to create the left-hand page.

Mini-Lesson

Comparing With Adjectives

Adjectives are used to compare two people, places, things, or groups. They are also used to compare more than two things.

- Add ***-er*** to most adjectives to compare two things.
- Add ***-est*** to most adjectives to compare more than two things.
- Use ***more*** and ***most***, not *-er* and *-est*, with long adjectives. Never use the words *more* and *most* with adjectives that already end in *-er* or *-est.*

Examples:	*light*	*light**er***	*light**est***
	sticky	*stick**ier***	*stick**iest***
	curious	***more** curious*	***most** curious*

How to Create Your Left-hand Notebook Page

Complete the following steps to create the left-hand page of your notebook.

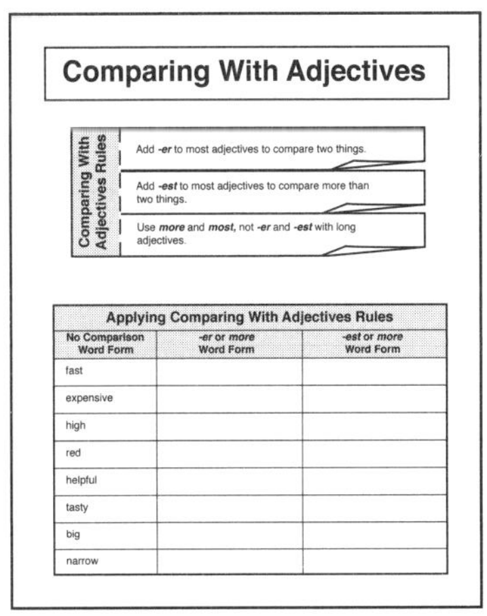

Step 1: Cut out the title and glue it to the top of the notebook page.
Step 2: Cut out the *Comparing With Adjectives Rules* flap book. Cut on the solid lines to create three flaps.
Step 3: Apply glue to the back of the gray tab and attach the flap book below the title. Under each flap, write an example sentence for the rule.
Step 4: Complete the *Applying Comparing With Adjectives Rules* chart. Cut out the chart and apply glue to the back. Attach it at the bottom of the page.

Demonstrate What You Have Learned

Think about the rules for comparing adjectives. In your interactive notebook, write four sentences of your own using the two words below. Use the *-er* and *-est* forms in two of the sentences and the *more* and *most* forms in the other two sentences.

1. tiny 2. helpful

Comparing With Adjectives

Comparing With Adjectives Rules	
	Add ***-er*** to most adjectives to compare two things.
	Add ***-est*** to most adjectives to compare more than two things.
	Use ***more*** and ***most***, not ***-er*** and ***-est***, with long adjectives.

Applying Comparing With Adjectives Rules		
No Comparison Word Form	***-er* or *more* Word Form**	***-est* or *most* Word Form**
fast		
expensive		
high		
red		
helpful		
tasty		
big		
narrow		

Student Instructions: Adverbs

Read the following information. Cut out the mini-lesson and attach it to the right-hand page of your interactive notebook. Use what you have learned to create the left-hand page.

Mini-Lesson

Adverbs

An **adverb** is a word that describes a verb, an adjective, or another adverb. Adverbs answer "how," "when," "where," or "to what extent." Many adverbs end with *-ly*.

Examples: *My aunt iced the cake smoothly.*
Smoothly tells how the cake was iced.

Tomorrow the play will end.
Tomorrow tells when the play will end.

Put the box here.
Here tells where to put the box.

Cathy was really surprised about the award.
Really tells to what extent Cathy was surprised.

How to Create Your Left-hand Notebook Page

Complete the following steps to create the left-hand page of your notebook.

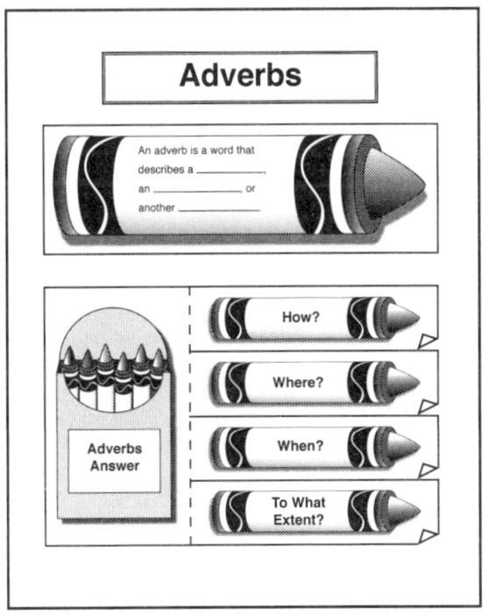

Step 1: Cut out the title and glue it to the top of the notebook page.
Step 2: Fill in the blanks on the large crayon piece. Cut out the piece. Apply glue to the back and attach it below the title.
Step 3: Cut out the *Adverbs Answer* flap book. Cut on the solid lines to create four flaps. Apply glue to the back of the crayon box tab. Attach the flap book at the bottom of the page.
Step 4: Under each flap, write a sentence using an adverb that answers the question.

Demonstrate What You Have Learned

Think about what you have learned about adverbs. In your interactive notebook, write a paragraph about an exciting event. Use at least three adverbs.

Adverbs

An adverb is a word that describes a ______________, an ________________, or another ________________.

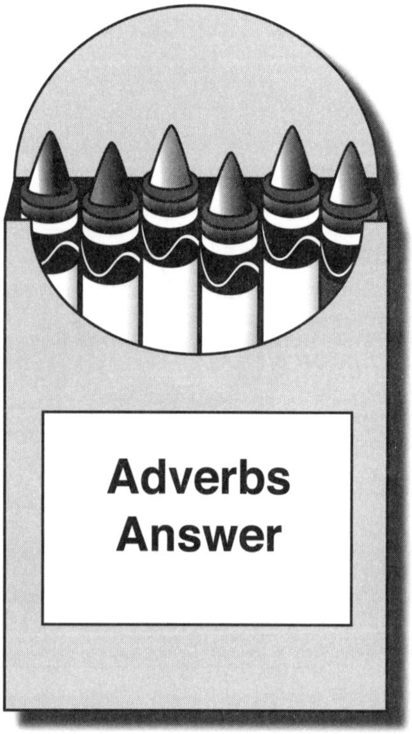

How?

Where?

When?

To What Extent?

Student Instructions: Comparing With Adverbs

Read the following information. Cut out the mini-lesson and attach it to the right-hand page of your interactive notebook. Use what you have learned to create the left-hand page.

Mini-Lesson

Comparing With Adverbs

When **adverbs** tell about verbs, they can be used to compare two or more actions.

- Use ***-er*** or ***more*** with an adverb to compare two actions.
- Use ***-est*** or ***most*** with an adverb to compare three or more actions.

Examples: *Ricky will finish his report soon.*
*Ricky will finish his report soon**er** than John.*
*Ricky will finish the soon**est** of all.*

- Use ***-er*** or ***-est*** with most one-syllable adverbs.
- Use ***more*** or ***most*** with many adverbs of two or more syllables.

Examples:	*late*	*lat**er***	*lat**est***
	excitedly	***more** excitedly*	***most** excitedly*

How to Create Your Left-hand Notebook Page

Complete the following steps to create the left-hand page of your notebook.

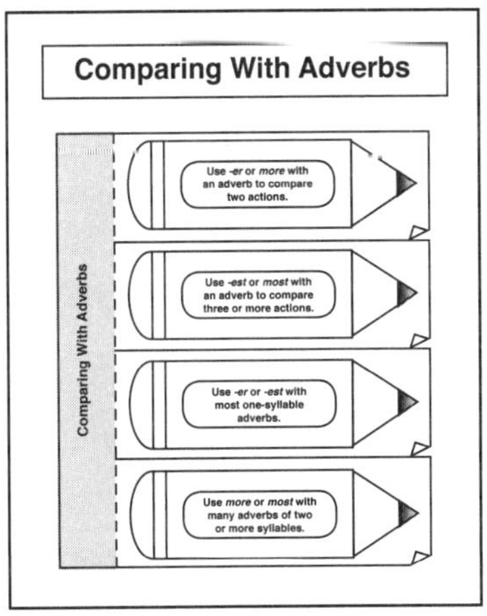

Step 1: Cut out the title and glue it to the top of the notebook page.

Step 2: Cut out the *Comparing With Adverbs* flap book. Cut on the solid lines to create four flaps. Apply glue to the back of the gray tab and attach the flap book below the title.

Step 3: Write a sentence under each flap that demonstrates the rule.

Demonstrate What You Have Learned

Draw the chart below in your interactive notebook. Complete with the correct adverb form.

Adverb	Compare Two	Compare More Than Two
fast		
kindly		
noisily		

Comparing With Adverbs

Comparing With Adverbs

Use *-er* or *more* with an adverb to compare two actions.

Use *-est* or *most* with an adverb to compare three or more actions.

Use *-er* or *-est* with most one-syllable adverbs.

Use *more* or *most* with many adverbs of two or more syllables.

Student Instructions: Prepositions

Read the following information. Cut out the mini-lesson and attach it to the right-hand page of your interactive notebook. Use what you have learned to create the left-hand page.

Mini-Lesson

Prepositions

A **preposition** shows the relationship between a noun or pronoun and another word in the sentence. The **object** of the preposition is the noun or pronoun that follows the preposition.

Example: *Linda placed it on the shelf.*
(on shows a relationship between placed and shelf.)
(on is the ***preposition****; shelf is the* ***object****.)*

Common Prepositions

to	*on*	*in*	*of*	*by*	*at*
by	*up*	*off*	*about*	*above*	*below*
under	*with*	*over*	*around*	*before*	*beside*
against	*down*	*from*	*out*	*into*	*after*
across	*onto*	*behind*	*near*	*until*	*without*

How to Create Your Left-hand Notebook Page

Complete the following steps to create the left-hand page of your notebook.

Step 1: Cut out the title and glue it to the top of the notebook page.

Step 2: Fill in the blanks on the *Preposition* flower piece. Underline the preposition and circle the object of the preposition in each sentence on the petals.

Step 3: Cut out the *Preposition* flower piece. Apply glue to the back of the gray center section and attach the piece below the title.

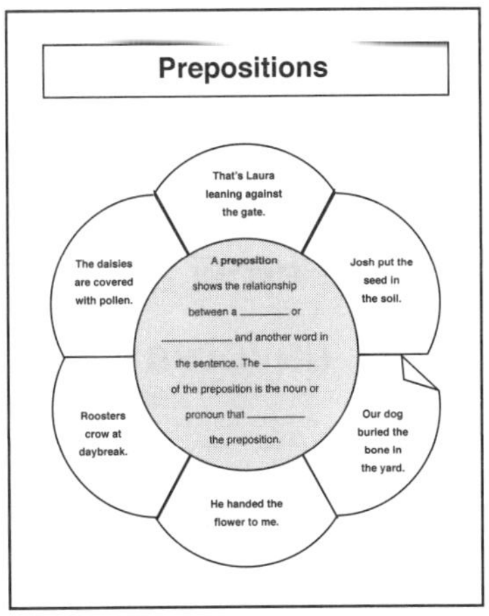

Demonstrate What You Have Learned

In your interactive notebook, use three prepositions to describe the location of another person in the room.

Prepositions

That's Laura leaning against the gate.

The daisies are covered with pollen.

A **preposition** shows the relationship between a __________ or __________ and another word in the sentence. The __________ of the preposition is the noun or pronoun that __________ the preposition.

Josh put the seed in the soil.

Roosters crow at daybreak.

Our dog buried the bone in the yard.

He handed the flower to me.

Student Instructions: Prepositional Phrases

Read the following information. Cut out the mini-lesson and attach it to the right-hand page of your interactive notebook. Use what you have learned to create the left-hand page.

Mini-Lesson

Prepositional Phrases

A **prepositional phrase** consists of a preposition, its object, and any words in between. A prepositional phrase ends with a noun or pronoun called the **object of the preposition**.

Example: *Axel placed it under the shelf.*
(under is the preposition; shelf is its object; the whole phrase tells *where* Axel placed it; therefore the phrase describes a verb.)

Prepositional phrases may be used to tell "where," "when," "how," or "which one." They may also describe a noun or pronoun.

Example: *The girl in the sweater left the building.*

How to Create Your Left-hand Notebook Page

Complete the following steps to create the left-hand page of your notebook.

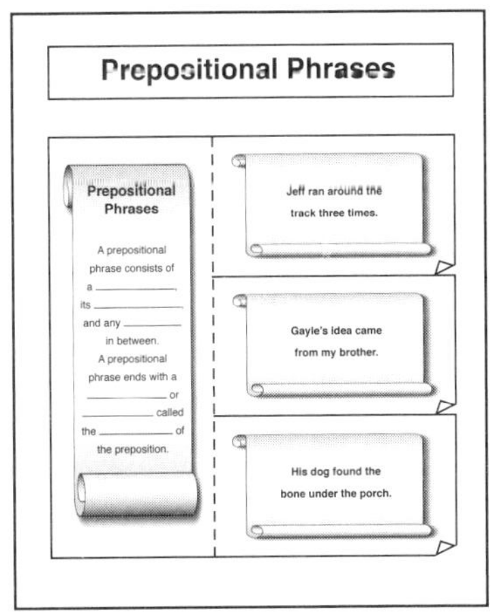

Step 1: Cut out the title and glue it to the top of the notebook page.

Step 2: Fill in the blanks on the *Prepositional Phrases* flap book.

Step 3: Cut out the *Prepositional Phrases* flap book. Cut on the solid lines to create three flaps. Apply glue to the back of the vertical *Prepositional Phrases* section and attach the flap book below the title.

Step 4: Circle the prepositions and underline the object of the preposition on each flap piece. Under each flap, write a sentence of your own that contains a prepositional phrase.

Demonstrate What You Have Learned

Think about how schools might change in the future. Write a paragraph in your interactive notebook explaining what schools might be like in 20 years. Use at least five prepositional phrases. Underline each phrase.

Prepositional Phrases

Prepositional Phrases

A prepositional phrase consists of a ______________, its ______________, and any ______________ in between. A prepositional phrase ends with a ______________ or ______________ called the ______________ of the preposition.

Jeff ran around the track three times.

Gayle's idea came from my brother.

His dog found the bone under the porch.

Student Instructions: Pronouns

Read the following information. Cut out the mini-lesson and attach it to the right-hand page of your interactive notebook. Use what you have learned to create the left-hand page.

Mini-Lesson

Pronouns

A **pronoun** is a word that takes the place of a noun or nouns. **Subject pronouns** are *I, you, he, she, it, we,* and *they.* Subject pronouns are used as subjects and after forms of the verb *be.*

Examples: *She lives next door.* (Subject pronoun)
My neighbor is she. (Follows a form of the verb *be* and means the same thing as the subject).

How to Create Your Left-hand Notebook Page

Complete the following steps to create the left-hand page of your notebook.

Step 1: Cut out the title and glue it to the top of the notebook page.

Step 2: Cut out the *Pronouns* flap book. Apply glue to the back of the gray center section and attach the flap book below the title.

Step 3: Cut out the five pronoun pieces. Apply glue to the back of each piece. Attach a pronoun to each flap.

Step 4: Under each flap, write a sentence using the pronoun.

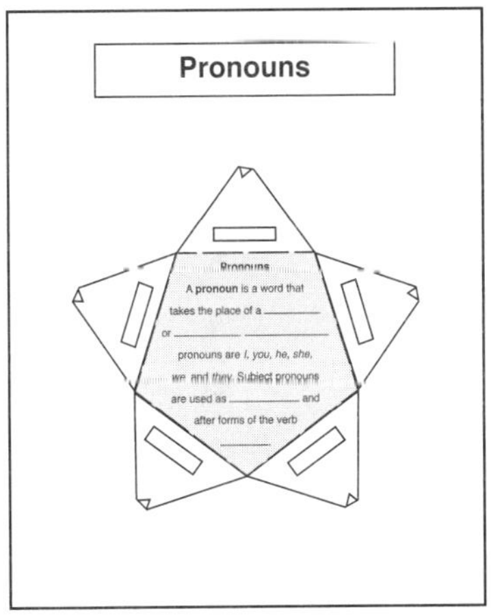

Demonstrate What You Have Learned

In your interactive notebook, write a paragraph about an activity you enjoy doing with your friends. Correctly use pronouns when writing about the activity. Underline all the pronouns that you use.

Pronouns

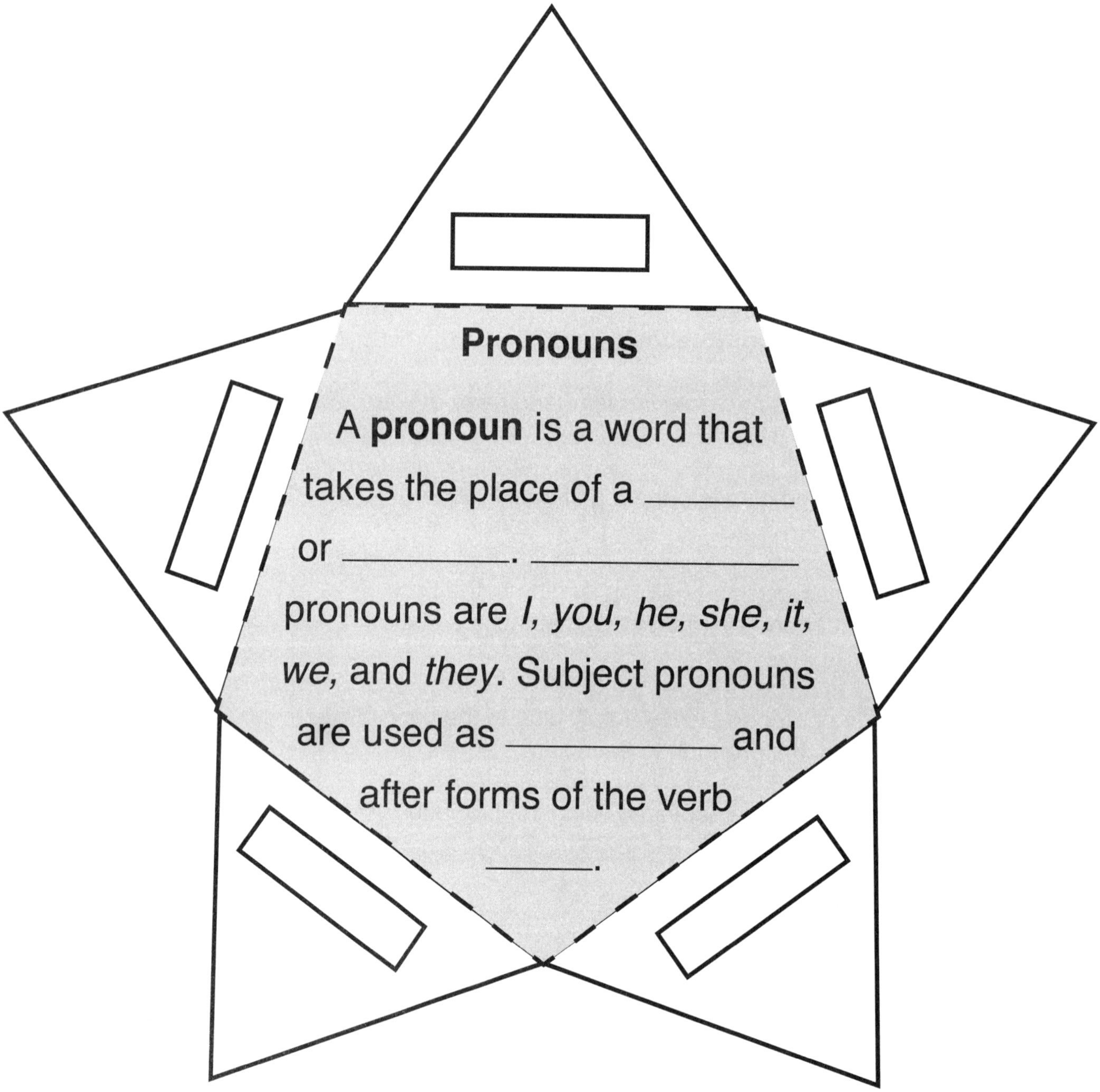

she		we
I	they	he

Student Instructions: Objective Pronouns

Read the following information. Cut out the mini-lesson and attach it to the right-hand page of your interactive notebook. Use what you have learned to create the left-hand page.

Mini-Lesson

Objective Pronouns

An **objective pronoun** is used instead of a noun; it is not the subject of the sentence. Objective pronouns are *me, you, him, her, it, us,* and *them.* Objective pronouns are used after action verbs and words such as *to* and *for. It* and *you* may be either subject or object pronouns.

Examples: *Aunt Joyce called her son. (noun)*
Aunt Joyce called him. (object pronoun)

You have a beautiful garden. (subject)
She gave you a seed catalog. (object)

How to Create Your Left-hand Notebook Page

Complete the following steps to create the left-hand page of your notebook.

Step 1: Cut out the title and glue it to the top of the notebook page.

Step 2: Cut out the four *Rule* flap pieces. Apply glue to the back of the gray tabs and attach each piece below the title.

Step 3: Under each flap, write a sentence that shows your understanding of the rule.

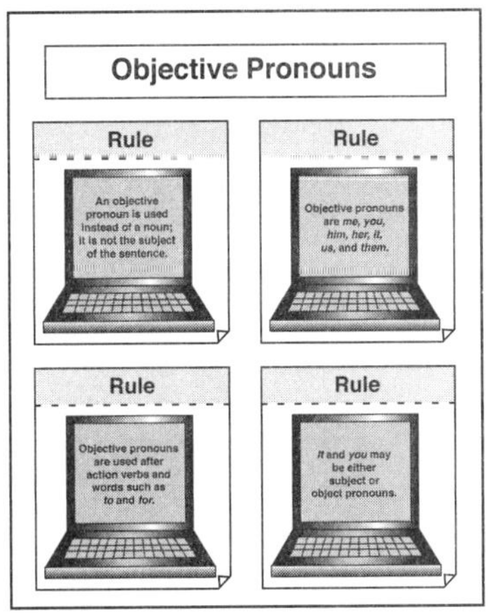

Demonstrate What You Have Learned

Think about the rules for using objective pronouns. In your interactive notebook, write a paragraph about pets. Then underline the pronouns.

Objective Pronouns

Rule

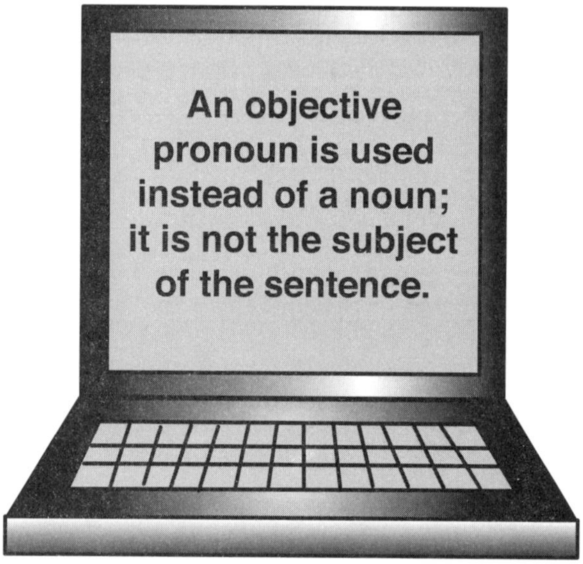

Rule

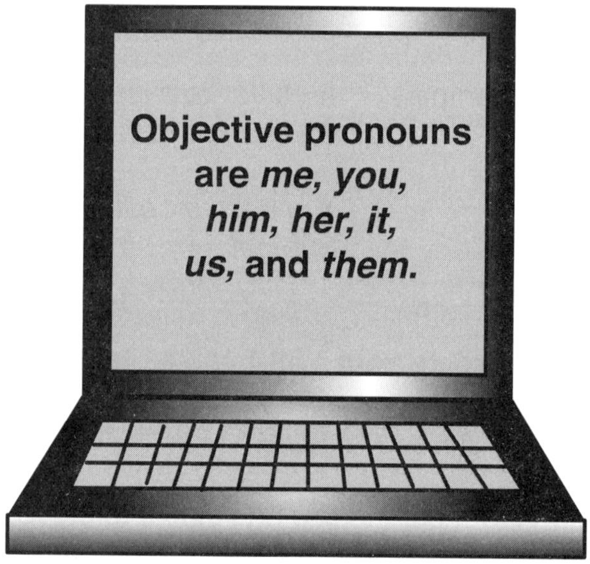

Rule

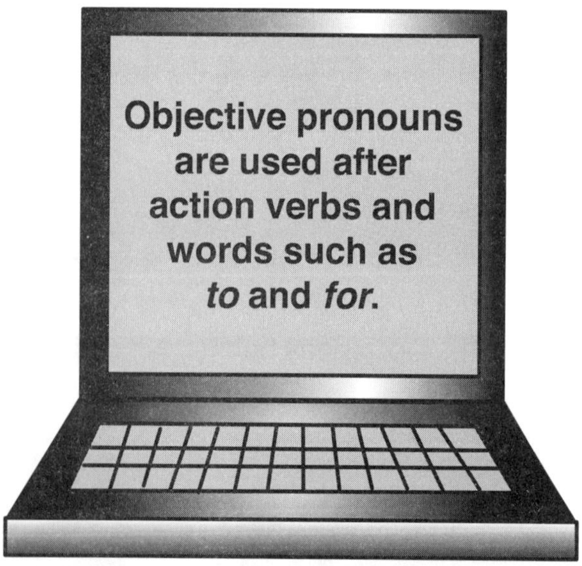

Rule

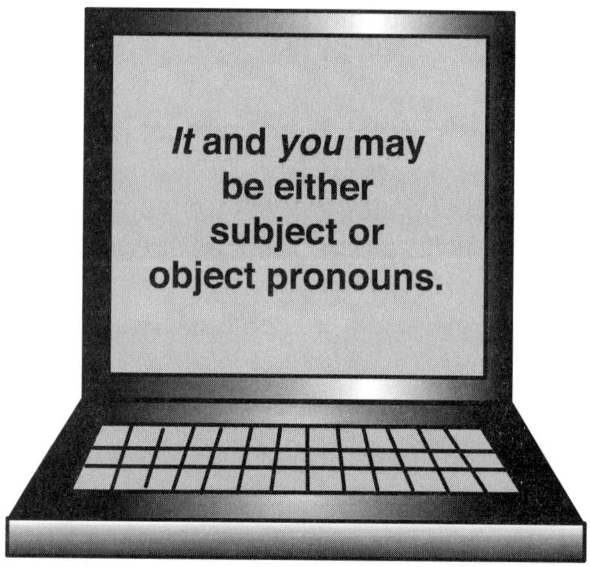

Student Instructions: Possessive Pronouns

Read the following information. Cut out the mini-lesson and attach it to the right-hand page of your interactive notebook. Use what you have learned to create the left-hand page.

Mini-Lesson

Possessive Pronouns

A **possessive pronoun** shows ownership. Use *my, your, his, her, its, our* and *these* before nouns.

Examples: *The team won* <u>*its*</u> *race.*
Gary held <u>*my*</u> *basketball.*

Use the possessive pronouns *mine, yours, his, hers, its, ours,* and *theirs* to replace nouns in a sentence.

Examples:	*(noun)* <u>*Sherry's pencil*</u> *is red.*	*(pronoun)* <u>*Hers*</u> *is red.*
	(noun) The basketball is <u>*Tim's*</u>*.*	*(pronoun) The basketball is* <u>*his*</u>*.*

How to Create Your Left-hand Notebook Page

Complete the following steps to create the left-hand page of your notebook.

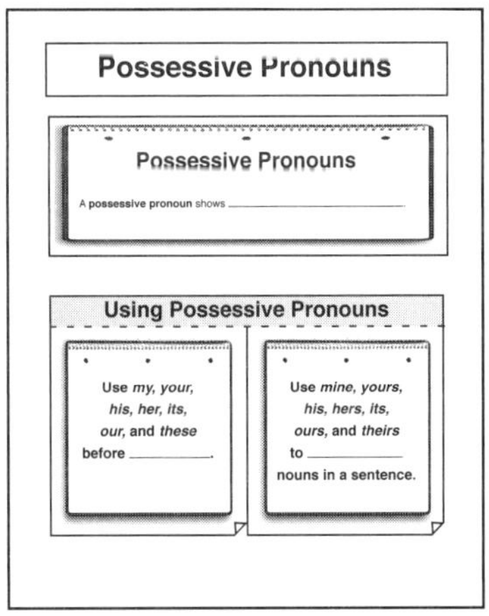

Step 1: Cut out the title and glue it to the top of the notebook page.

Step 2: Fill in the blank on the *Possessive Pronouns* piece. Cut out the piece. Apply glue to the back and attach it below the title.

Step 3: Fill in the blank on each *Using Possessive Pronouns* flap piece. Cut out the piece. Cut on the solid line to create two flaps. Apply glue to the back of the gray tab and attach the piece at the bottom of the page. Under each flap, write a sentence that demonstrates the usage.

Demonstrate What You Have Learned

Fill in the blank with the correct possessive pronoun in the sentences below. Then copy the sentences below in your interactive notebook.

1. James thought ____________ (him, his) outfit looked terrific.
2. Do you know if that book is ____________ (my, mine)?

Possessive Pronouns

Possessive Pronouns

A **possessive pronoun** shows ________________.

Using Possessive Pronouns

Use *my, your, his, her, its, our,* and *these* before ____________.

Use *mine, yours, his, hers, its, ours,* and *theirs* to ____________ nouns in a sentence.

Student Instructions: Capitalization

Read the following information. Cut out the mini-lesson and attach it to the right-hand page of your interactive notebook. Use what you have learned to create the left-hand page.

Mini-Lesson

Capitalization

Capital letters are used for the first word in all sentences and the word *I* whatever its position in a sentence. A capital letter also signals the first word in a direct quotation.

Examples: *Strong wind made it difficult to play outside. (first word in a sentence)*
I played basketball before I left high school. (pronoun I)
James asked, "Has anyone seen my dog?" (first word in quotation)

Capitalize **proper nouns** and **proper adjectives**.

Examples:	Common Noun	Proper Noun	Proper Adjective
	country	*England*	*English*

How to Create Your Left-hand Notebook Page

Complete the following steps to create the left-hand page of your notebook.

Step 1: Cut out the title and glue it to the top of the notebook page.

Step 2: Cut out the *Capitalization Rules* flap book. Cut on the solid diagonal lines to create four flaps.

Step 3: Apply glue to the back of the gray center section and attach the flap book below the title.

Step 4: Under each flap, write a sentence to demonstrate the rule.

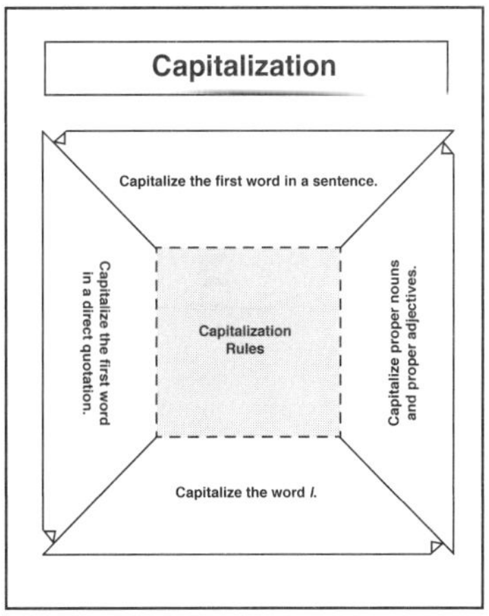

Demonstrate What You Have Learned

Think about the rules for capitalization. In your interactive notebook, write a short conversation you had with someone today. Correctly use capitalization in your direct quotes.

Capitalization

Capitalize the first word in a sentence.

Capitalize the first word in a direct quotation.

Capitalization Rules

Capitalize proper nouns and proper adjectives.

Capitalize the word *I*.

Student Instructions: Commas

Read the following information. Cut out the mini-lesson and attach it to the right-hand page of your interactive notebook. Use what you have learned to create the left-hand page.

Mini-Lesson

Commas

A **comma** (,) is a punctuation mark used to separate items in a **series**. Put a comma after each item except the last one. Use *and* or *or* before the last item in a series.

Examples: *The zoo animals included lions, tigers, bears, and monkeys.*
Give the basketball to Tom, Connor, or Melissa.

A comma is used following **introductory words** such as *yes, no, oh,* and *well.*

Examples: *Oh, I didn't see you there.*
Well, that's all right.

A comma is used to set off **nouns of direct address**, the name of the person being directly spoken to.

Examples: *Susan, place these books on the shelf.*
I'm not sure, Grandma, if I want fish or chicken.
Your car is ready, Mr. President.

How to Create Your Left-hand Notebook Page

Complete the following steps to create the left-hand page of your notebook.

Step 1: Cut out the title and glue it to the top of the notebook page.

Step 2: Cut out the *Comma Rules* flap book. Apply glue to the center section and attach the flap book below the title.

Step 3: Under each flap, write a sentence demonstrating the comma rule.

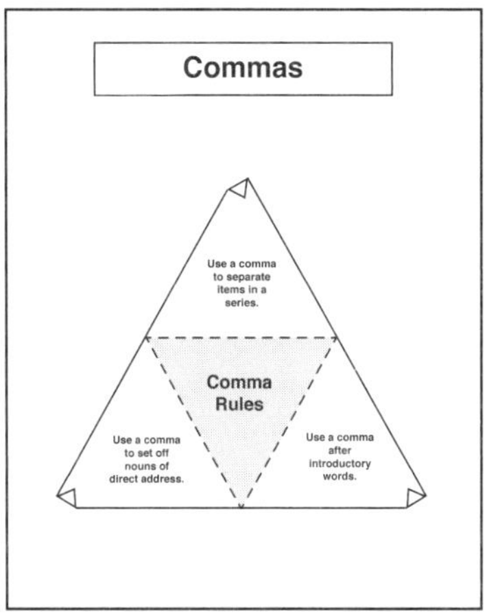

Demonstrate What You Have Learned

Think about what you have learned. Look in your favorite fiction book for sentences using each of the comma rules. Write the title of the book in your interactive notebook. Copy the sentences below the title of your book.

Commas

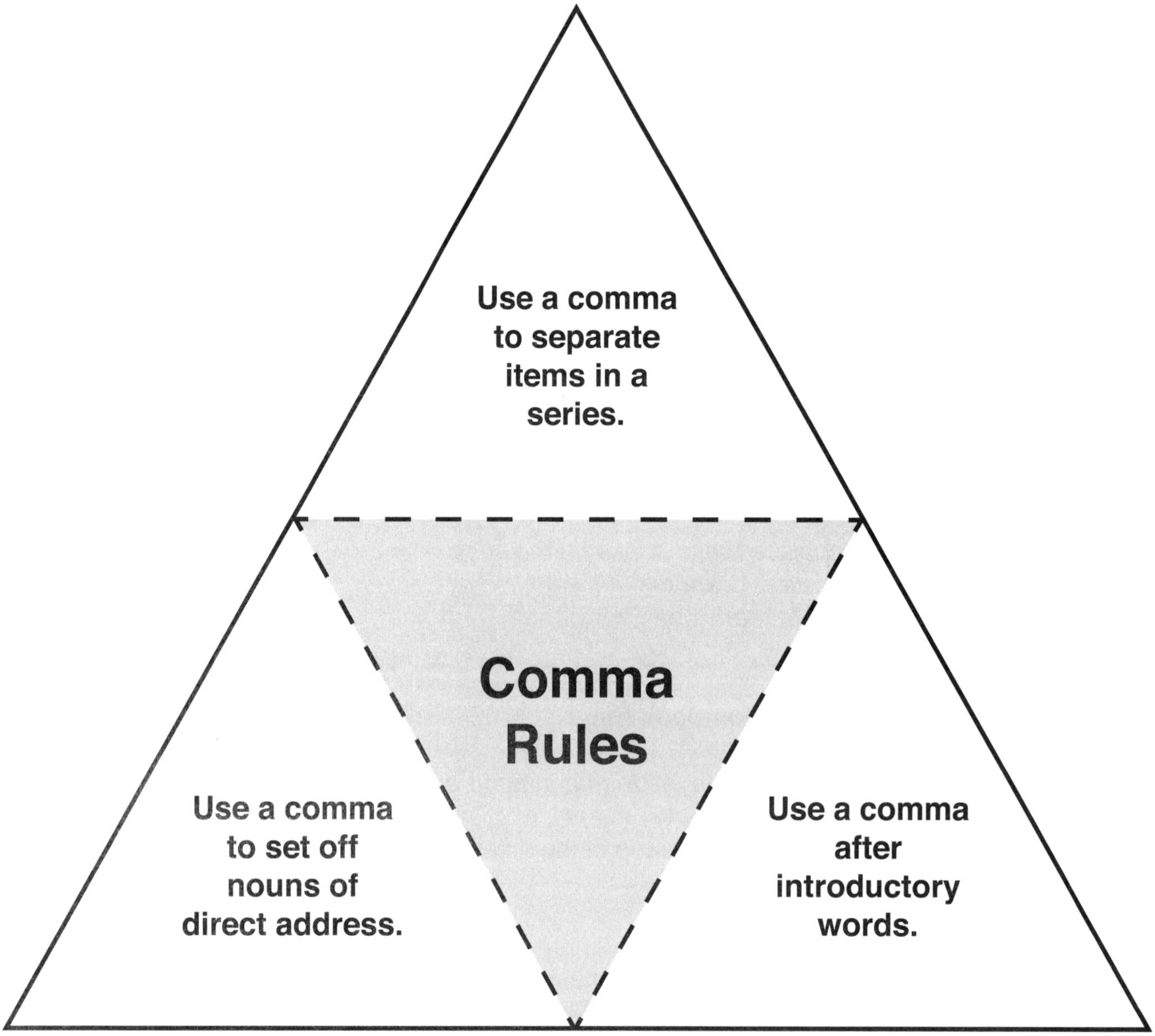
Use a comma to separate items in a series.
Comma Rules
Use a comma to set off nouns of direct address.
Use a comma after introductory words.

Student Instructions: Capitalization and Punctuation of Titles

Read the following information. Cut out the mini-lesson and attach it to the right-hand page of your interactive notebook. Use what you have learned to create the left-hand page.

Mini-Lesson

Capitalization and Punctuation of Titles

Capitalize the first, last and all important words in a title. **Underline** the titles of books, magazines, newspapers, television shows, and movies. (In printed text, these titles would be in *italics*). Put quotation marks (" ") around titles of short stories, songs, articles, book chapters, and most poems.

Examples: (article) "**A L**ook at **B**irds"
(book) **A F**ox at **M**idnight

Capitalize the first letter of a person's title used with their name. When a title is used with the words *a, the,* or a possessive pronoun (*my, our,* and so on), do not capitalize it.

Examples:	Our guest was **M**ayor Russell.	Our guest was ***a*** mayor.
	I asked **M**om a question.	***My*** mom left early.
	Dr. Harris sat in a chair.	***The*** doctor gave a shot.

How to Create Your Left-hand Notebook Page

Complete the following steps to create the left-hand page of your notebook.

Step 1: Cut out the title and glue it to the top of the notebook page.

Step 2: Fill in the blanks on the four *Rule* flap pieces. Cut out each piece. Apply glue to the back of the gray tabs and attach the pieces below the title.

Step 3: Under each flap piece, write an example demonstrating the rule.

Demonstrate What You Have Learned

Think about the rules for capitalization and punctuation of titles. Look in your favorite fiction book or newspaper for the use of each rule. Write the title of the book or newspaper in your interactive notebook. Copy the sentences below the title.

Capitalization and Punctuation of Titles

Rule

Capitalize the first, ____________, and all ________________ words in a title.

Rule

__________________ the titles of books, magazines, newspapers, television shows, and movies.

Rule

Put ________________ marks around titles of short stories, songs, articles, book __________, and most poems.

Rule

Capitalize the ______________ letter of a person's ______________ used with their name.

Answer Keys

Answers are limited to those not presented as part of the mini-lessons on each "Student Instructions" page.

Imperative Sentences

Left-hand Page (p. 8)

Go to the game.
Don't make these mistakes.
Remember to set the alarm.
Follow instructions.
Rent the video game at the store.
Go to science class.

Complete Subjects and Predicates

Student Instructions (p. 9)

1. My sister has the flu.
2. The Norton family is vacationing in New York.

Left-hand Page (p. 11)

Identifying Complete Subjects and Predicates:

complete predicate
complete subject
complete subject
complete predicate

Compound Subjects and Predicates

Left-hand Page (p. 12)

Compound Subjects: Neither chips nor sodas are healthy after-school snacks.
The window or door has to be closed.
Brian and Kendra went to the beach during spring break.
Compound Predicates: The team worked and finished their science project.
Marie always laughed or cried at dramatic plays.
Steve competed but lost the race.

Common and Proper Nouns

Left-hand Page (p. 16)

Common Nouns: woman, town, cat, restaurant
Proper Nouns: Pacific Ocean, Blue Mountains, Pizza Place, Spanish

Plural Nouns

Student Instructions (p. 17)

1. desks 2. pianos 3. leaves

Possessive Nouns

Student Instructions (p. 19)

pony's, ponies, ponies'

Left-hand Page (p. 20)

family's, families, families'
child's, children, children's
goose's, geese, geese's
trout's, trout, trout's
teacher's, teachers, teachers'

Nouns as Objects

Student Instructions (p. 21)

1. Tony (S), accepted (A.V.), trophy (D.O.)
2. caterpillars (S),make (A.V.), cocoons (D.O.)

Left-hand Page (p. 22)

catcher (S), shortstop (I.O.), ball (D.O.)
Dr. Chen (S), son (I.O.), bike (D.O.)

Predicate Nouns

Left-hand Page (p. 24)

volunteers (P.N.), are (L.V.)
teacher (P.N.), was (L.V.)

Answer Keys (cont.)

Helping and Linking Verbs

Left-hand Page (p. 28)

1. Helping Verb
2. Linking Verb
3. Helping Verb
4. Linking Verb
5. Linking Verb
6. Helping Verb
7. Helping Verb
8. Linking Verb

Contractions

Student Instructions (p. 33)

1. Manuel didn't call me last night.
   did call
2. I don't like watermelon.
   do like

Adjectives/Proper Adjectives

Student Instructions (p. 35)

Russian, Danish, Alaskan, Turkish, Greek or Grecian

Comparing with Adjectives

Student Instructions (p. 39)

Sentences will vary.

1. tinier, tiniest
2. more helpful, most helpful

Left-hand Page (p. 40)

faster, fastest;
more expensive, most expensive;
higher, highest;
redder, reddest;
more helpful, most helpful;
tastier, tastiest;
bigger, biggest;
narrower, narrowest or more narrow, most narrow

Comparing with Adverbs

Student Instructions (p. 43)

fast: faster, fastest
kindly: more kindly, most kindly
(or kindlier, kindliest)
noisily: more noisily, most noisily

Prepositions

Left-hand Page (p. 46)

(clockwise from top)

against gate
in soil
in yard
to me
at daybreak
with pollen

Prepositional Phrases

Left-hand Page (p. 48)

around track
from brother
under porch

Possessive Pronouns

Student Instructions (p. 53)

1. his
2. mine